Unclenching
Our Fists

9/19/13

for Bonnie,

I honor your tremendous courage,
your unshakeable strength.
your bright spirit
and loving heart.

It has been an honor and privilege to be by your side.

Toward a nonviolent future!

Sara

Unclenching Our Fists

Abusive Men on the Journey to Nonviolence

Sara Elinoff Acker

Photography by Peter Acker

Vanderbilt University Press

NASHVILLE

© 2013 by Vanderbilt University Press
Nashville, Tennessee 37235
All rights reserved
First printing 2013

This book is printed on acid-free paper.
Manufactured in the United States of America

Library of Congress Cataloging-in-Publication Data on file
LC control number 2013002806
LC classification HV1441.8.U5E45 2013
Dewey class number 362.82'9286—dc23

ISBN 978-0-8265-1941-2 (cloth)
ISBN 978-0-8265-1942-9 (paperback)
ISBN 978-0-8265-1943-6 (ebook)

In memory of my father, Saul Elinoff,
who showed me from the start
what a safe and loving man can be. . . .

Contents

Unclenching
Our Fists

Introduction

We clench our fists in a moment's notice,
but unclenching them is another matter.
> —Anna Politkovskaya, the Russian journalist who reported
> on the Chechnya war and was shot to death outside her
> Moscow apartment in 2006.

FOR MY COLLEAGUES AND me in western Massachusetts, the late 1980s through the mid-1990s was a devastating time to work with families affected by domestic violence. There had been an unprecedented string of domestic violence murders: over the course of eight years, ten women and one child had been killed. One was particularly horrific. Sherry Morton and her eighteen-month-old son, Cedric, were stabbed to death by Sherry's ex-boyfriend, the baby's father. The entire community was traumatized.

In the wake of these murders, the community became determined to create a more coordinated and collaborative system to try to reduce the risk of lethal violence. Spearheaded by the District Attorney's office, key players in the community—police officers and dispatchers, prosecutors and probation officers, advocates and batterer intervention counselors—collaborated to create a more seamless response to families affected by domestic violence. One of the people at the table was Yoko Kato, the mother and grandmother of Sherry and Cedric. A local dressmaker who decades earlier had come to the United States from her native Japan, Yoko forged her grief over their murders into a commitment to work as a domestic violence activist.

Yoko knew that helping survivors wasn't enough. She realized that no matter how many victims were helped, the source of the problem was the men who were abusive and violent. She yearned to understand how to stop men's violence. This is what brought her to Men Over-

1

coming Violence, the batterer intervention program where I worked, part of the Men's Resource Center for Change in Amherst, Massachusetts. Yoko joined our board of directors.

It was Yoko's idea to dialogue directly with some of the men enrolled in our program. She wanted the opportunity to ask domestic violence perpetrators some difficult questions. Why did they feel justified hurting their partners? What excuses did they make for their behaviors? How did they learn to be violent? What got them to wake up and face themselves? She also wanted to share her story, the story of Sherry and Cedric and her work as an activist. We arranged a meeting one November afternoon in 1997 with Yoko, five members of our group program, several of our counselors and our program director.

It had been four years since Sherry and Cedric had been killed. My colleagues and I were nervous. We had never seen anything like this before: a survivor and perpetrators sitting in a room together, speaking directly to one another. I had worked in battered women's programs for more than a decade before becoming the partner support counselor at Men Overcoming Violence. In all my years doing domestic violence work, there was always a firewall between domestic violence victims and perpetrators. Unless they were in a courtroom, survivors and perpetrators were never intentionally brought into the same space.

Healing, possibility, and hope can show up in the most unlikely of places. The meeting that day was one of those places. Our small meeting room was crowded, buzzing with tension. At Yoko's invitation and with the permission of the participants, the entire dialogue was being filmed by a Japanese television crew. In addition to her work as a local activist, Yoko was taking domestic violence prevention work back to Japan, where the issue was an enormous problem with scant awareness or resources to address it. The footage from the meeting was going to be part of an expose on domestic violence, offering the first glimpse many Japanese citizens would have of domestic abuse perpetrators talking about their violence.

The men who participated in the meeting that day had been invited to attend by program staff because they had shown promise. Each had acknowledged responsibility for his violence and had been attending our program for at least two years. Each also agreed to share his story with Yoko.

Because there was no place left to sit, I stood in the doorway. While Yoko shared her story, the men listened attentively. Her voice broke when she described her daughter and grandson, what they were like while they were alive, and her relationship with them. She spoke of Sherry's abusive relationship, her struggle to break away, and the trauma of their violent deaths. She talked about her feelings about the perpetrator, sitting in jail after being found guilty of their murders. Finally, she spoke about her mission to end the violence that took the lives of her daughter and grandson. The room was so still I could hear my own breathing.

One by one, the men began to tell their stories. They talked about the abuse they had perpetrated against their partners and the damage their behavior had caused. They talked about getting arrested or being served restraining orders and what it had taken to finally get them to take responsibility for what they had done. They talked about the work they were doing in our program. Each voiced his regrets; some choked back tears. They seemed to sense how deeply Yoko was listening, sharing with her both their deep remorse and the pride they felt about their small successes. They shared with her the wounds they were working to heal and, most significantly, the different men they were becoming. Yoko challenged the men to continue their work *and* to reach out to other men who had violence and abuse problems.

Yoko told me later that the meeting was an important turning point in her own healing process. Though the man who murdered Sherry and Cedric was in prison, he continued to be unremorseful. By contrast, the men who shared their stories had taken responsibility for their violence. This was important for her to witness. "I wanted to see if some of these men—if they got the right intervention and support— could really end their violence," she told me. "It's too late for Sherry and Cedric, but the work you are doing might help save someone else's children and grandchildren."

When I first started working in the field of domestic violence, I didn't believe abusive men could really change. Now I know that some can. Sadly, men who've committed to change are only a small minority of men who are abusive. Too many abusive men continue to live unrepentant lives, unaccountable, still a danger to their families. The men whose stories you will read are part of a select group chosen by batterer intervention program leaders from around the country as representatives of the best possible outcome: men who have faced themselves and stopped their abusive behaviors. Many of them did not choose to enroll in their programs, but ultimately each *did choose* to become nonviolent. It is my hope that their stories will inspire others to make the same choice.

A caveat: The stories in this book are those of heterosexual men who were abusive to their female partners. It's important to recognize that domestic violence is a huge concern in lesbian, gay, and transgender communities, where it appears to occur at similar rates as in heterosexual relationships. In addition, there is increasing awareness of women who are perpetrators. However, the vast majority of domestic violence victims continue to be women abused by their male partners, according to Department of Justice statistics.[1] This book's focus reflects that reality.

The men in *Unclenching Our Fists* tell about the abuse they perpetrated and how eventually they had to face the consequences of their behaviors. They recount their early days in their programs, and the ways their thinking and behavior started to change. They talk about the damage they caused, the relationships that cannot be repaired, and the guilt and sorrow they carry. They reveal what allowed them to go deeper into the painful, liberating work of self-examination and the supports that kept them going. Many talk about the roots of their violence, in their experiences as children and in the messages they received about manhood and masculinity. A few are still with the partners they once abused; for most, their abuse destroyed their relationships.

The men in this book, like abusive men everywhere, used to blame their partners for their behavior. They also blamed their drinking, or their childhoods, for their actions and attitudes. Eventually, each came to recognize that no one else makes them act abusively; their behavior is always their own choice. Although each has done significant work in stopping his violence, they all understand they must continue to be vigilant if they want to stay abuse-free. Each understands there may still be issues to work on; the process is never perfect and it is never over.

The men decided to share their stories because they want to help other men who struggle with abuse. It is no small thing to "come out" publicly as a recovering abuser, especially since I asked if I could include their photographs with their story. The photographs are important because they show that men who struggle with abuse look just like many of the men in our lives. They are white, black, Asian, and Latino; laborers, artists, accountants, physicians, police officers. They are our husbands and fathers, sons and brothers, neighbors and friends. The photographs are intended to show each man's humanity *and* to remind us that most abusive men are not monsters: they are good men who have serious problems with anger, control, and violence.

Two men chose to share their stories but not their photographs; both requested pseudonyms. They requested anonymity out of a concern for potential negative consequences in their communities. Their need to conceal their identities illustrates the stigma men face when they publicly acknowledge their abuse and violence. A third man agreed to have his photograph published but asked that his real name not be used.

Men with abuse problems need to know that other men have faced their own violence and that change is possible. Unfortunately, many abusive men never seek help or even recognize that their behavior is damaging to their partners and children. Even when they attend intervention programs, many don't take the work seriously. But for those who make a heartfelt commitment to examining themselves, these stories of awakening and taking responsibility can offer a template of the process of individual change.

What Follows in These Pages

The first chapter takes us into the world of batterer intervention, offering vignettes from the work and discussing the larger controversies and questions surrounding our efforts to hold abusers accountable and to help them change. I share my own journey from being a victim advocate to a batterer intervention counselor and how my ideas about abusive men changed over time. This is followed by the stories of eleven men who've committed to nonviolence.

The stories in *Unclenching Our Fists* were gathered over eight years. I began by interviewing men from my own program, then reached out to other programs across the country. I conducted most of the interviews over the telephone; some were face to face. After the interviews were transcribed, I edited them into the stories you will read. I interviewed twenty-five men and chose eleven stories that reflect a diversity of men who've been abusive and violent. Each man included in the book reviewed his own story for accuracy. Whenever possible, I verified each man's continued nonviolence through contact with his current partner.

Following the stories, Chapter 2, "The Road to Nonviolence," examines some of the common steps men take as they come to terms with their abuse and transform their behavior and beliefs. It describes specific features of the journey to nonviolence, sharing markers of both progress and backsliding. This chapter also offers guidance for men trying to make amends with their partners and children. It discusses accountability and the complexities of repairing relationships where there has been abuse.

The next chapter, "When the Man You Love is Abusive," is written for women partners. While I hope many abusive men will read this book, I realize many women experiencing abuse will be reading it as well. This chapter offers some tools women readers can use to assess whether their partners are really committed to change. It also discusses important ways women can get support and take care of themselves.

The book concludes with "The Last Word: Domestic Violence Survivors and Advocates Respond." This chapter is an account of a focus group of seven survivors and three advocates and describes their mixed reactions to the stories in *Unclenching Our Fists*. Because abused women bear the ultimate price of intimate partner violence, I wanted the book to end with their voices.

The Larger Picture

I wrote this book because I believe that stories of abusive men who have become nonviolent are important and need to be more widely known. At the same time, it is critical that these stories be viewed in context. Even though the men in this book have made profound changes, we must never forget that they still leave behind a legacy of damaged lives. Their wives, former partners, and children may still carry the scars of abuse.

Every week when I facilitated my batterer's intervention group, I always tried to remember the people who weren't in the room: the women and children who'd been harmed. As you read the stories and look at the photos of the men in this book, I hope you'll remember the women and children just outside the frame.

The roots of domestic violence lie in the larger social norms and inequities in our society: sexism, the promotion of violent masculinity, inequality, and the idea that violence is an acceptable way to resolve conflict. Given the magnitude of the social and cultural forces that underlie domestic violence, some might think that stories of individual perpetrators who've changed are mere anecdotes rather than pathways to change.

I disagree. Individual stories advance our understanding of how to build a nonviolent world, showing us the insights and actions necessary on a personal level. We make change in our world on both a larger structural level *and* one individual at a time. We need both. When men who've been abusive speak out in their communities about their past violence, we begin to see the potential role they can play as ambassadors of change.

Balancing Hope with Caution

One of the biggest concerns some battered women's advocates raised about publishing stories like these is that they might kindle an unrealistic sense of hope among women experiencing domestic violence. This is a legitimate concern: abused women do stay in their relationships longer out of hope their partners might change. In many cases, this hope only increases their danger of being abused.

Yet more and more advocates now understand that many battered women do *not* want to end their relationships—what they want is for their partners to end their violence and abuse. A powerful way to respond to that hope is by providing real stories of men who've worked hard to change their beliefs, attitudes, and behaviors; stories that show the amount of time and commitment it takes to overcome violence.

I am deeply grateful to the men I interviewed for so openly sharing their lives with me. I appreciate the courage they have shown in their willingness to be public. They understand that some people will respond to their stories with anger and suspicion. Nevertheless, they've chosen to share their stories out of the hope that other abusive men will follow their example and commit to nonviolence.

If you're a man who's just admitted to yourself that you are abusive, this book is for you. Find a group of other men who share your struggle and start the work. You owe it to the people you love, and to yourself. You can choose to unclench your fists.

CHAPTER 1

Working with Abusive Men

EVERY THURSDAY EVENING, TWELVE men file into the small, cluttered group room where I work. They sit on a variety of old, mismatched furniture—second hand couches and folding chairs—coffee cups and slices of pizza in hand. They range in age from their early twenties into their sixties. Some look nervous or preoccupied, others are relaxed and bantering with the men who sit near them. The men span a diverse spectrum of occupations and incomes: a real estate agent sits next to an unemployed roofer; the landscaper sits between a PhD student and a cab driver.

These men's lives probably never would have overlapped were it not for one thing they have in common: they have all abused the women they loved.

Soon the casual conversation winds down and our group begins. "How did your week go?" my co-facilitator asks. "Did you have any incidents of abuse? Were you able to prevent yourself from having any incidents?" One by one the men "check in"—talking about their efforts to remain nonviolent during the previous week. One man says he's worried about going to court on a year-old domestic violence charge. Another discusses a tense email exchange with his ex-partner over child visitation. A third man admits he raised his voice and swore at his partner.

The men are dropping into the work of the evening. Everyone in the room is there because he has been physically violent, intimidating, and threatening, or emotionally and verbally abusive to his partner. The mission of the group is to encourage each man to face his problems and learn how to stop his abuse. The twelve men in our group are not alone. Every week, in an estimated fifteen hundred locations across the country, men are meeting in similar batterer intervention groups.

Batterer intervention programs were founded in the United States beginning in the 1970s, working with both mandated and self-referred clients. The first programs for male batterers were established in Seattle, Denver, and Cambridge, Massachusetts. Today, there are programs in all fifty states and many countries around the world. They offer a combination of didactic teaching and personal exploration with the goal of ending intimate partner abuse. Programs vary in length, most from twenty-six to fifty-two weeks, depending on state standards. Groups are run by trained facilitators, usually male-female pairs, in part to model a healthy, respectful, and egalitarian working relationship between a woman and a man.

Batterer intervention groups, at their best, create a space where men acting abusively can take responsibility for their behavior, recognize the impact of their actions on their families, and learn to become non-violent. Group members are taught practical skills to help them interrupt their own abusive behavior. They are challenged to address not just their angry and physically violent episodes but also their ongoing patterns of control and emotional abuse. They are taught how to interact with partners in egalitarian, noncontrolling ways and how to parent nonviolently.

In addition, batterer intervention programs can be a source of important information for victims, probation departments, and referral sources. Programs share information about group members' attendance and level of participation, as well as flagging potential problems, including dangerousness. Often this helps guide decisions about sentencing, whether an abusive man should have contact with his children, and whether he needs to address other problems such as substance abuse, mental health, and parenting. By reporting any indicators of potentially dangerous behavior or resistance to taking responsibility for past violence, batterer intervention programs provide critical information to courts, child welfare departments, and victims.

My own program, Men Overcoming Violence, is one of sixteen certified batterer's intervention programs in Massachusetts. Over the course of two decades, Men Overcoming Violence (now called the

Moving Forward program) has worked with close to three thousand men. At its peak, our program ran eleven weekly groups in the four western counties of Massachusetts, including one for inmates in the county jail.

Men come to our program because their domestic abuse has been met with some kind of consequence: their wives or partners have decided to leave; they've been arrested for domestic assault and battery; or child protective services got involved with the family and required them to attend a program. Sometimes men call us in the aftermath of a horrible incident when they feel ashamed of what they've done. No matter what the circumstances, most men start attending because some kind of crisis has awakened them—at least temporarily—to an important truth: their abusive behavior is unacceptable.

No one is born abusive. Abusive attitudes and behaviors are learned and, with great diligence, can be unlearned. But before abusive men can change, they need to stop blaming everybody else—wives, girlfriends, parents, bosses, the world at large—for their behavior. They must recognize that their abuse is traumatizing to their partners and children. For there to be any possibility of change, they must first admit that they alone are responsible for their abuse. Such accountability represents an enormous shift in how they think about the violence; many abusive men never take that step.

For many years when people would ask about my work, they'd often say, "I've heard that abusive men really don't change. Isn't it frustrating and hard to work with men like that?" The work *is* sometimes frustrating, and it certainly *is* difficult; change doesn't come easily to abusive men. But what I've seen is that some men who have been abusive *do* become nonviolent. I think that the transformation these men make is among the most underreported stories in the field of domestic violence.

Addressing Domestic Violence: A Historic Crossroads

Domestic violence has been an epidemic in our society for generations. For centuries it has been shrouded in secrecy and, if acknowledged at all, kept private, a family matter. Traditionally, since women were often seen as the property of their husbands and had significantly less power, politically and economically, those who experienced abuse in their homes were expected to tolerate the behavior. This remains true in many parts of the world today.

Although great progress has been made in the United States in the last generation, domestic violence continues to be a deadly problem, with women as the primary victims. Department of Justice statistics from 2004 show that in the 625,000 cases of intimate partner abuse reported to law enforcement, eighty-five percent of the victims were women.[1] Seventy-five percent of the perpetrators were men.[2] Although the number of men being assaulted is rising (most likely due to an easing of the stigma around reporting), in 2010 women were still four times more likely to be the victim of intimate partner violence than men.[3]

Most domestic violence incidents are not reported to the police; reported incidents of assaults represent only the tip of the iceberg. Most experts believe that only one in ten incidents is reported to law enforcement. This means that as many as twelve million individuals may be involved each year in domestic violence incidents as victims and perpetrators.

Domestic violence is part of my own family's history. For more than sixty years, my grandmother was emotionally abused. My grandfather ruled the roost. If my grandmother, my mother, and her two sisters didn't do as he wished, he verbally lashed out at them. He controlled every aspect of their lives. He was especially cruel to my grandmother, flaunting mistresses, never expressing affection or telling her he loved her. Instead he was demeaning and critical almost every day of their decades-long marriage. My grandmother became depressed, would refuse to eat, and was hospitalized at different times throughout her life. My mother begged her to leave the marriage, but my grandmother was economically dependent and afraid to be on her own.

There was barely any language to describe what my grandmother was going through—words like "domestic violence" or "emotional abuse" were not yet part of anyone's vocabulary. She wasn't being beaten, so no one would ever see her experience as legitimate abuse.

Her experience was simply understood as the way marriage is, something to endure "for the sake of the children." Throughout her marriage, my grandfather was never held accountable.

With the rise of the second wave of the feminist movement in the late 1960s, things began to change. Feminist activists and domestic violence survivors started organizing for the right of women to live lives free of abuse. The silence surrounding family violence was finally broken.

Domestic abuse, activists proclaimed, is not simply an "anger issue." Feminists were the first to articulate that domestic abuse is *about power*. They defined it as a pervasive pattern of dominance and control in which one person in a relationship consistently uses intimidation, threats, control, and blame to manipulate the other. Physical violence is only one dimension of the problem and isn't used by all abusers. Domestic violence also includes emotional and economic abuse, sexual abuse, and the manipulation of children.

Feminists argued that rather than looking toward psychological causes, domestic violence should be understood as a societal problem, reinforced by deeply held cultural beliefs rooted in sexism. When you consider that for centuries women have been second-class citizens, that men are considered the undisputed rulers of their families, that violence is seen as an acceptable way to express anger or resolve conflict, and that power is defined by the amount of control one has over others, then violence against women inevitably follows. To end domestic violence, feminists asserted, the status of women and girls must be transformed, traditional notions of masculinity must be challenged, and power must be redefined.

The second wave of feminism gave birth to consciousness raising groups where women met together to explore the way sexism impacted their personal lives. As women talked about the violence in their intimate lives, they began to see just how widespread these problems were. It was most likely the first time in history that terms like "wife abuse," "battering," "incest," and "sexual abuse" entered the national conversation and were taken seriously as social problems. Feminists established safe homes for women fleeing domestic violence. In 1974, the first battered women's shelter in the U.S. opened in Minnesota. Within three years there were nearly ninety shelters for battered women across the country. Today, more than two thousand shelters and support organizations for victims of domestic violence are operating in the United States.

These battered women's programs saved thousands of lives by providing abused women and their children with shelter, counseling, and advocacy. Despite many successes, too many women still continued to be brutalized, some killed, at the hands of their partners. It was clear that programs for victims were not enough. Activists realized that successfully combating domestic violence would require new programs to intervene with abuse perpetrators. Additionally, intimate partner violence needed to be criminalized. New laws were created so arrests could be made based on probable cause (rather than a police officer being required to witness a violent incident.) Protective orders became easier for victims to obtain, and violation of those orders resulted in criminal charges. Police, judiciary, clergy, and health care workers received critical training. Primary prevention programs in schools and community education campaigns were established. Fundamentally, services for victims and their children became part of an overall web of response to the problem of domestic violence. Activists helped to keep the momentum going for this ever-expanding social change effort, in a coordinated community response.[4]

A critical component of this response was intervention with perpetrators. No matter how many battered women's programs were established, no matter how many women and children were helped, the plague of domestic violence would continue unabated until abusers stopped perpetrating their violence. Somebody had to work with the men, to interrupt the violence and abuse and teach alternative behaviors. This is where programs like the one where I worked came in.

What's a Nice Feminist Like Me Doing in a Place Like This?

In my early years working with battered women, if someone had told me I would someday be involved in trying to help abusers or writing a book like this, I would have been incredulous. Like many other women working in domestic violence programs, I firmly believed that abusers could not change; that they would never voluntarily give up the benefits of power and control over their families that battering afforded them. I was convinced that the only way an abused woman could be safe was by leaving her batterer. I believed that if society really wanted to stop domestic violence, the best use of energy and resources was helping women escape from abusive relationships. I considered it my duty to help abuse victims see this and help them get out of their destructive relationships.

Over my many years in this work, my perspective on this has shifted. It remains true that some relationships are so dangerous that our efforts must be directed at keeping victims safe and getting perpetrators incarcerated. It is also true that there is no hope of change if a perpetrator refuses to take responsibility for his behavior. But there are other situations when abusers can learn nonviolence by participating in abuse intervention programs. I have come to see that for some families, change is possible. To explain why my thinking has changed, I'd like to share a little of my own story.

In 1985 I took a job at "Women Helping Battered Women," an agency in Burlington, Vermont, offering crisis intervention, counseling, advocacy, a children's program, and a confidential shelter. I was twenty-six years old, passionately committed to the movement to end violence against women. I worked as one of two crisis intervention coordinators for the program. My job was to answer the hotline, taking calls from women in danger. In addition to intervening in crises and training volunteers to do the same, I offered women individual counseling and ran support groups.

I had become a feminist in college, and, as a women's studies major, educated myself about issues of violence against women. But nothing in my student years could have prepared me for the raw emotion I felt answering crisis calls and bearing witness to the terror battered women were enduring. I will never forget the sound of the women's panicked voices when they called our hotline, or the looks on their faces when they showed up at our shelter in the middle of the night with hastily packed suitcases and bewildered children.

I remember a call from a woman locked in her bathroom, terrified that her raging husband was going to break down the door. While I tried to help her stay calm, a coworker called the police. The husband was arrested. Another time, late one night, I worked with a woman I'll call "Holly" who, just a couple of hours before, had been beaten by her boyfriend. She arrived at our shelter door straight from the hospital emergency room. Her face was swollen, covered in bruises; her eyes were narrow slits from having her head slammed repeatedly into a car dashboard. I sat with her for hours as she cried. Later, I found out I knew her abusive boyfriend—he was a former colleague of mine at a progressive newspaper where I had worked as a journalist. My ideas about what type of men are abusive was shattered: I understood that even so-called "liberal, enlightened" men could batter their partners.

A few months later I started working with "Laurene," who had been in an abusive marriage for fifteen years. She and her husband got into a terrible fight and he started beating her. He hit her over the head with a framed mirror, fracturing her skull. Then he dragged her into their car and started driving toward a nearby forest. Terrified he was going to kill her, Laurene pleaded with him to take her instead to the hospital, promising she wouldn't say he had beaten her. He agreed. In the emergency room, a savvy nurse took one look at Laurene and separated her from her husband. In a private exam room, she asked Laurene if her husband had beaten her. When Laurene nodded mutely, the nurse called the police; her husband was arrested.

Laurene's legal case made the headlines. Everyone in our agency supported her through the long court process and was with her the day her husband was sentenced to fifteen years in state prison for attempted murder. When Laurene walked out of the courtroom the day her husband was convicted, she was unafraid for the first time in years. She could finally begin the slow, painstaking process of putting her life back together. Laurene was just one of many women our agency helped leave their abusive relationships.

In 1988 I moved to western Massachusetts to pursue a master's degree in social work. After graduating, I worked as a clinician in a community mental health center. But domestic violence work was still my passion, so when a job opened up at a local battered women's agency,

I applied. I was hired to work as an individual and group counselor in a former mill town entrenched in poverty, child abuse, and domestic violence.

While I was working at my new job, I started hearing about a local program for domestic abusers called Men Overcoming Violence (MOVE). It was part of an organization called the Men's Resource Center (MRC), whose mission was to support men, challenge men's violence, and develop men's leadership. The MRC was started by a group of men whose lives had been transformed by feminism. They had been examining the way their own lives had been narrowly constricted by rigid ideas about what it meant to "be a man." They decided to create an organization where men could come together to support one another and challenge men's violence against women.

Intrigued, I met with some of the men who worked as counselors in the batterer intervention program. For the past year, they had been running a group for men who were abusive and controlling with their partners. Ten men attended the group, all of them by choice. The counselors offered education about domestic abuse, behavioral strategies for stopping violence, and discussions about men's socialization.

As I listened to the counselors from the MRC talk about their work, I was immediately struck by how deeply they seemed to understand the pain and suffering battered women experience. They made no excuses for the behavior of the men in their group. They were committed to confronting them and holding them accountable for their abuse. The work was very hard and slow going, they said, but a few of their group members were really showing some promise. Some of the original group members had decided to continue meeting even though their twenty-six-week basic program was complete. I was surprised to hear about their commitment—it was beyond anything I could have ever imagined.

A few months later, I had the opportunity to meet with a batterer intervention group member. My first husband was working on a short documentary for a PBS television series called *The '90s*; one program was addressing the topic of violence. We decided to collaborate on a piece about domestic abuse, highlighting the Men Overcoming Violence program. We contacted the program director and asked if we could interview one of the men he had talked about, one who was taking responsibility for his behavior. Did he think a group member would be willing to "go public" and discuss his abuse before a national broadcast television audience? I was almost certain the answer would be "no." To my surprise, he gave us the phone number of a man named Scott.

Scott and his wife Nancy had been married for nearly twenty years and had four sons, ages twelve to sixteen. Scott had been abusive in his family for most of that time. He'd been attending his group at the MOVE program for a year; both he and his wife were willing to be interviewed about his domestic abuse.

We drove to their house on a blustery winter day just after an enormous snowstorm. We decided to interview them separately—to give each a chance to speak freely and without fear. We spent six hours in their home, listening to each of them talk about how Scott's abuse had devastated their marriage and impacted their children. They also spoke about the changes that were starting to happen.

It was the first time I had ever heard an abusive man be accountable for his behavior, talking openly about the damage he had caused. Scott spoke candidly about his angry outbursts: the shoving, arm grabbing, destruction of property, and other intimidating behaviors he used. He offered no superficial explanations, no excuses, no minimizing, no rationalizing. I could sense his remorse as he spoke. Scott had much to reckon with. He was beginning to understand how much he had damaged his family's love and trust. As he faced himself more honestly each week in his group, he became more anguished as he recognized the impact of his abuse. Considering everything I knew about men and domestic violence, I thought he might have quit looking at himself, but so far, he hadn't.

Nancy corroborated Scott's account. She said the work he was doing in group was starting to have an impact on their marriage. For the first time in nearly twenty years, she didn't have to hide her feelings or walk on eggshells around him. She was hopeful that Scott was starting to turn things around—not only stopping his abuse, but perhaps starting to become a different kind of man.

Yet while Scott attended his group, Nancy remained totally isolated. She had tried earlier to get support from the local battered women's shelter, but they recommended she leave the marriage. I winced when I heard this—how many times had I said the same thing? Nancy got me thinking about what happens when that advice, no matter how well meaning, is out of step with where a woman is in her life. If someone like Nancy thinks that the people she has turned to for support will judge her for waiting to see if things can change, why would she continue to seek help from them?

Nancy told me she wished she could talk to the other wives of the men in Scott's group. She wondered if those women were experiencing improvements at home, like she was. She wondered how they were handling their own emotions, all the pent-up grief and anger. Were they as worried as she was that their husbands would cycle back into abusive behavior? How would any of them know whether the changes would be lasting?

As I listened to Nancy, a light bulb switched on in my head. I understood what she needed—a safe place to talk and understanding people to talk with. She needed a place where she could get more information and where she wouldn't be judged. I had spent years running groups for women whose partners were not interested in getting help. Didn't the women whose partners were in batterer intervention also deserve support? The next day, I asked the director of the program if I could help create a program for Nancy and the other partners. His response was an enthusiastic yes.

This is how I became the first female staff member of Men Overcoming Violence. In addition to my job at the battered women's program, I worked six hours a week as the "Partner Contact Counselor" at MOVE. I reached out to every woman whose partner or ex-partner was enrolled to see what concerns or questions she might have. I provided information about the MOVE program's curriculum and goals. I created a brochure that answered many important questions that partners had, including signs of progress and backsliding. I learned more about their experiences of the abuse and the kind of changes they were hoping for. Some partners welcomed ongoing support so I kept in regular contact with them while their husbands and boyfriends progressed through the program. I made sure every woman knew about the more comprehensive services offered at their local battered women's program. When a few expressed interest in meeting other wives, I started our first partner support group, beginning with Nancy and seven others.

The meeting with Scott and Nancy that winter's day had opened up a completely new direction for my work. Yet it was only the first of two profound experiences I had that year that led me to re-examine some of the ideas I had about domestic violence perpetrators and ultimately changed the course of my activism.

One of my clients at the battered women's program was a woman named "Tricia," a mother of two and a victim of her husband's ongoing emotional abuse. After meeting with me for several months, Tricia got up the courage to challenge her husband, "Phil." When he became threatening with her, she responded by taking out a restraining order against him. Phil left their home and went to live with his mother.

A few weeks later, Phil's mother called Tricia, saying that he was depressed and was threatening to kill himself. Tricia discussed this in our next session; she was very worried. Should she take him back? But I knew that abusive men often threatened suicide to manipulate their partners into reconciling. We did a safety assessment and some safety planning together. The best thing Tricia could do, I counseled, was to keep the restraining order in place and hope that his family would insist Phil get help.

One week later, Tricia got a call from the state police informing her that Phil had killed himself. Tricia was bereft and I was horrified. It made no sense, I told myself. He could have addressed his abusive behavior. At my job at Men Overcoming Violence, men just like Phil were getting help. Many of them had far more severe patterns of abuse than he did. Why hadn't he even tried?

A couple of days after his suicide, I went to a staff meeting at the battered women's program. Word had gotten out among my coworkers about my client's situation and I was looking forward to having some time at the meeting to process this difficult event. I expected my colleagues to be troubled about the situation, especially about the burden of guilt my client was now going to carry and the impact on her daughters. I expected that other staff would share my feeling of the waste and tragedy of it all.

Some did. But for a few, the suicide provoked a really different response. One of my coworkers commented, "Well as far as I'm concerned, that's just one less batterer on earth to terrorize women." A few other staff members nodded their agreement. I was shocked by her comments; I didn't know what to say.

I left the meeting and sat in my car so I could be alone. Yes, Phil had been abusive, I said to myself, but that didn't mean he deserved to die. He had needed help. He had needed to find another way to live—without inflicting violence on his family or on himself. But instead, his suicide had traumatized his whole family, and now two little girls would grow up without their father.

In that conversation, I felt an enormous chasm open between my coworkers and myself. Though I understood their anger at the violence abusers perpetrate, I was upset that they could be so cavalier. They believed that abusive men were irredeemable. But were they? I thought about my conversation with Scott in his kitchen. I thought about Phil. What could have been done to give Phil the same chance that Scott had?

After Phil's suicide, I knew I wanted to do more to help abusive men get the help they needed, to prevent more tragedies like this from occurring. I decided to immerse myself in the work at the men's center. I was able to expand my hours running the partner support program and received training to become a certified batterer intervention counselor.

My New Role as a Batterer Intervention Counselor

My early days of working directly with abusive men were riddled with frustration. It felt so difficult to "get through" to the men, to help them really understand the impact of their behavior. I'll always remember "Jamey," a member of the one of the first groups I cofacilitated. Jamey was in his early twenties, though he looked no older than sixteen. He worked part time as a mechanic in an auto shop. Jamey had been arrested for domestic assault and battery against his girlfriend and mandated to our program. He'd only been coming to our group for a few weeks and was a reluctant participant, sitting mostly mute with his baseball cap pulled low over his face.

One particular evening Jamey spoke up more than he ever had. It was the week before Christmas and he was upset that because of a restraining order, he wasn't going to see his two young children over the holiday. He told the group how much he missed his kids and then blamed his girlfriend for "keeping me from seeing them." I interrupted him. "Is it your girlfriend's fault that you're not seeing your boys?" I asked him. "Why don't you spend a little time thinking about why she got the restraining order in the first place? Isn't it your own behavior that created this situation?" Jamey didn't respond and looked away. He didn't say another word the rest of the night.

I had been facilitating these groups for just under a year but I carried with me ten years of hearing the stories and pain of abuse victims. I was often angered by what group members said. I understood intellectually that it can take abusive men a long time to accept full responsibility for their behavior. But I found it very difficult, emotionally, to hear their rationalizations, blame, and denial. I noticed that my more seasoned colleagues seemed to possess a patience that I hadn't yet cultivated.

During staff meetings, we would discuss clients like Jamey. How long should we allow him to go on before challenging him? If what we are saying, even if accurate, causes him to shut down and shut us out, is that an effective intervention? My colleagues believed that making compassionate connections with the men in our groups would give us more ability to challenge them. Yet as a former advocate, I worried: is this the best strategy to help the men change their behaviors and attitudes?

Our program wasn't the only one with internal debates. It seemed the entire field of batterer intervention was filled with conflicting ideas about how to challenge men's abuse and violence. Even today, close to forty years after the first programs opened in the United States, there is still a lack of consensus about how to hold men who batter accountable, how to measure program effectiveness, and how to understand the ultimate causes of men's abusive behaviors. Additionally, there are debates about the overall role of batterer intervention in the larger criminal justice response to domestic violence.

Similar Goals, Different Strategies

Most intervention specialists agree on certain fundamental goals when working with abusive men. These include

- Insisting that men take full responsibility for their actions, understanding that their behavior is always a choice
- Helping men see that abuse includes emotionally abusive and controlling behaviors as well as physical violence
- Teaching strategies for de-escalation
- Offering alternative ways of handling conflict and difficult feelings
- Helping men understand the impact of their behavior on their partners and children and develop empathy

Where programs disagree is how to accomplish these goals. Which curriculum is the most effective? What tools are most useful for interrupting violence? How do we dismantle denial? Is it important to explore men's own exposure to violence and abuse or will that reinforce their sense of victimhood? Is the goal simply to hold men accountable for their abuse or are we trying to help them become different kinds of men?

At the heart of our disagreements is the question about why some men become abusive. Many programs cite sexism and gender roles. Others give more consideration to individual factors: psychological makeup, the influence of family of origin, exposure to violence in childhood. Some programs try to integrate the two, bringing together the personal and the political.

Sexism's Role in Domestic Violence

The central role of sexism in granting men power and control in their intimate relationships—and the way that fosters abuse—has guided much of the work of batterer intervention programs across the country for several decades. Sexism teaches boys and men to devalue and objectify women, to feel entitled to dominate their intimate relationships and to use violence and control to maintain their power. Not only do many men learn that abuse and control over their intimate partners is normal, but that by dominating and objectifying women, they will get respect from other men. Therefore, challenging men's sexism and entitlement, or "male dominance," was seen as central to the work of batterer intervention.

Though this remains an important explanation for why partner abuse occurs, many intervention practitioners have come to realize that male dominance cannot be the *sole* explanation for the violence in our clients' lives. There are too many situations where it does not adequately explain intimate partner abuse, for example, in the lesbian and gay community or by women toward men. Even with heterosexual male perpetrators, our program's experiences working with abusive men revealed that while ideas about dominance and entitlement were important, there were many other things going on in the life experience and mindset of a man who uses violence.

In addition, sexism's impact on the men in our groups was more complex than simply grooming them for dominance and exploitation. Some of our group members did behave like stereotypical chauvinists and "tough guys," treating their partners terribly out of the belief they had the right to dominate and abuse them. But others did not fit this profile. Their abuse seemed to be motivated more by fear or insecurity than any need for dominance. We realized that while sexism does teach men to disrespect or dominate women, this was only part of its impact. The other side of the sexism coin is that by demanding allegiance to a very narrow code of manhood, men's emotional lives and ability to have healthy relationships are often damaged.

As boys grow up, the dominant culture pressures them to be "tough guys," while simultaneously demanding their emotional repression. Men are supposed appear strong and in control all of the time, regardless of what is happening for them. The only emotion that is ever permissible is anger. Showing fear or vulnerability isn't "manly"; these feelings need to be stuffed inside. Boys who express these more tender feelings are often bullied and ridiculed.

We suggested to the men in our groups that sexism not only damages the way they view women, it damages them as well. We introduced the idea of the "Man Box"—the very narrow range of behavior they had to conform to in order to be seen as "real men." What were their experiences of feeling pressured to "act like a man?" What were the consequences if they didn't act tough or manly enough? Almost every man in our program had a story to tell. Some had distinct memories of being shamed by family members if they cried or showed any fear. Others recalled times when they'd be subjected to taunting, bullying, or even violence for not acting "manly." A few of the group members admitted that they were the ones doing the bullying of the guys who were "sissies."

We wanted to help the men in our program explore the dilemmas and privileges that sexism brought to their lives in its entirety: how it grooms them for violence on the one hand while closes them off to many parts of their full humanity on the other; how it encourages sexual objectification while at the same time creates emotional dependence on women. We believed that this more complex understanding of sexism's impact would be more effective than talking only about "male dominance."

Is it any wonder, we asked them, that many of their relationships with women were disastrous? On the one hand, they'd been trained to objectify women and to use control and abuse as a way to maintain power. On the other hand, they had few, if any, emotional skills or emotional self-awareness—vital for a healthy relationship. Was it possible that sometimes they resorted to abuse because they were asserting their dominance, and other times it was because didn't know any other way to express feeling scared, confused, lonely, jealous, or sad?

The pressure to "act like a man" ripples through men's lives in multiple ways. Not only does it impact their relationships with women, but it affects their friendships with one another. We talked about the competition and posturing that goes on among men, their reluctance to be vulnerable with each other, and how this contributes to their isolation and their dependence on women. We talked about how "acting like a man" meant punishing their bodies and pushing through pain, their lack of self-care, and why men have a high incidence of heart disease and stroke. In fact, we concluded, male socialization impacts *every-thing*—from men's relationships with their fathers to their relationships with women; from their roles as fathers to their friendships with other men; and the discomfort they felt exploring their inner lives. As important as this more complex understanding of sexism is though, it can *never* be an excuse for abusive behavior.

Individual Factors that Contribute to Violence

Even with the double bind sexism creates for men, the majority of men do not end up perpetrating abuse. It's essential to understand, then, what makes some men more likely to become abusive than others. Unfortunately, a more nuanced understanding of individual risk factors has been beyond the scope of many batterer intervention programs.

For some activists and practitioners, even considering family history, trauma, addiction, or mental health was viewed as a dangerous diversion, undermining the goal of helping men take responsibility for their violence. They were concerned this approach would reinforce men's sense of victimhood and become an excuse for their behavior. While I agree it is critical that abusive men understand that their behavior is always a choice, helping them understand all the contributors to their violence can make our work more effective.

Many programs around the country have begun to incorporate mental health and substance abuse assessments into their work. Some programs have also included a trauma-informed perspective. For many years, in most batterer intervention programs, even mentioning trauma was considered taboo. Yet ignoring trauma was like ignoring the elephant in the room.

A majority of men in batterer programs witnessed domestic violence growing up. Some experienced serious neglect or abuse at the hands of family members. Others were exposed to or participated in gang violence. Some were refugees from conflict or war zones. What we now understand is how trauma conditions these men for a life of distrust and hypervigilance.

Some of the men in our own program had experienced so much violence they were ready, at a moment's notice, to escalate if they felt attacked. Even routine disagreements with their partners put them into an immediate "fight or flight" response. As group leaders, we thought it was critical to help our clients understand if there was a connection between their early experiences of trauma and their current behavior. At the same time, we reminded them that many trauma survivors do not use abuse in their intimate relationships. The bottom line was that they were still giving themselves permission to act abusively.

When I would meet with other program leaders from around the country, I saw that they were also developing a more multidimensional understanding of abusive men. Many had come to the same realization: focusing on the dominance and privilege conferred by sexism, while important, was not comprehensive enough. But striking a balance between sexism's role in men's violence and individual factors based on family background, trauma exposure, substance abuse, and mental health remains delicate. The field continues to have a very vigorous discussion about program approaches, and there are heated disagreements. This debate is healthy. As our understanding of men's abuse and the best ways to intervene continues to evolve, this benefits both abuse perpetrators and victims.

Cultural and Economic Influences on Men's Violence

Not only sexism, but cultural and racial contexts have a significant influence on abusive behavior. Over the years, many batterer intervention programs became more culturally competent, understanding that interventions with a Latino, African-American, or Asian man couldn't be the same as with a white, middle class man. Program curricula needed to include the impact of racism on men's lives. We recognized that abusive men from minority communities can simultaneously be both victims and perpetrators of oppression.

The stressors of poverty and homelessness also contribute to men's abusive behavior. I remember when a client revealed he'd been sleeping in his car ever since his wife took out a restraining order. How could we talk to him about his past abuse when he hadn't eaten all day? Unless programs take into account clients' economic circumstances and make referrals to the services to help them, we will be hampered in our efforts to change abusive behavior.

Compassionate Confrontation

Not only did the *content* of our work with men have to become more comprehensive, but the *process* of intervening was just as important. Our program's approach was to balance confrontation with support. Psychotherapists understand that clients cannot make progress if they don't feel connected to and cared for by the therapist. But all too often intervention programs working with abusers left out the caring aspect, focusing only on the task of confronting behavior. We believed that most group members shut down in an environment that is overly critical.

The bottom line message we had for the men in our groups is that they were fundamentally good people engaging in completely unacceptable behaviors. We talked about abuse as something they do, not something they are. We tried to create a group culture where men supported and challenged one another. We described this approach as "compassionate confrontation"—holding men accountable for their behavior without shaming them and offering support without colluding with them.

Men were often surprised by the experience of support in our groups; most expected to be treated harshly. In this environment, over time, many were able to reveal more about the ways they had abused others. In the end, we believed that far more progress was made with a carrot than with a stick.

These ideas only represent my program's approach. There are many who will disagree with what I've written. The debate about best practices with abusive men continues. Currently, there is a strong push for more evidence-based practice as we continue to search for the most effective interventions with abusers. Even though there is no consensus, most practitioners now understand that a "one size fits all" approach to intervention is usually not effective. To help men change, programs have to be able to see each abusive man as both an individual and as part of a larger culture and to offer interventions that address the complexities behind his behavior.

Batterer Intervention: The Big Picture

As batterer intervention work evolves, the alarming fact remains that the vast majority of men arrested on domestic assault charges are still not even required to attend these programs. Judges cite cost and mixed reviews about program effectiveness.

Batterer intervention programs are costly because they are lengthy; most require anywhere from twenty-six to fifty-two weeks of attendance. Consequently, many judges send domestic violence offenders to shorter, less expensive anger management programs. But anger management programs are the wrong place for domestic abusers, for many reasons. Domestic abuse is an issue of power, not simply an issue of anger. By focusing exclusively on controlling rage and strengthening coping strategies, many anger management programs overlook other serious problems of coercion and control. Additionally many anger management programs ignore the larger context of sexism and how this influences abusive behavior. Most do not assess for lethality or have any kind of partner contact. Many domestic violence activists, concerned about this trend of replacing batterer programs with anger management, have been proactively educating judges about the difference between the two.

In other situations, domestic violence perpetrators with addiction issues are sometimes mandated by judges to substance abuse treatment but not domestic violence programs. While some substance abuse programs do address domestic violence, most do not. Most agree that abusers with substance abuse issues have two problems and need both addiction treatment and domestic violence intervention.

Additionally, there is an ongoing debate about the quality and effectiveness of the batterer programs themselves, another reason why abusive men are not more consistently referred. Although many activists in the movement to end domestic violence have high regard for batterer intervention programs, some view these programs as a waste of resources, even potentially dangerous to victims. Some programs have mixed reputations in their communities. Though many states have certification standards, there is no unifying national standard or philosophy of intervention. There are many different kinds of programs operating around the country, using a wide variety of intervention strategies and curricula with abusive men. But which types of interventions are the most effective? Many look to research to give a clearer picture of the effectiveness of batterer programs. But over the years, as long-term studies have been published, even the research has been controversial.

What Does the Research Show?

As of 2012, there have been about forty published studies of batterer intervention programs. The results vary widely: some conclude that batterer programs have a measurable impact; others say they do not.

Some argue that the different results have to do with the way the research was conducted. There are different kinds of research: most study the outcomes of individual programs (individual outcome studies); others compare the outcomes of abusers who complete programs with those who do not (quasi-experimental studies). A third group (experimental) compares violence rates among men who are randomly assigned to different intervention strategies. Each type of research has methodological weaknesses.

For example, some studies are only able to measure recidivism in re-arrest rates—which leaves out many incidents of physical abuse not reported to the police. Most studies do not measure emotional abuse at all, considered by many victims to be as devastating as physical violence. Many studies don't include reports from "partner contact"— acquiring perspective and information from a man's wife or girlfriend. Studies also have not included longer-term programs that work with abusers beyond forty or fifty-two weeks.

Many experimental research studies conclude that there are few measurable differences between offenders who attend batterer intervention programs and those who don't. A study by Dr. Julia Babcock of the University of Houston concluded these programs have a "minimal impact of reducing recidivism beyond the effects of being arrested."[5]

But other quasi-experimental research shows that batterer programs do reduce recidivism in two-thirds of men who complete them (especially over a period of time), and that men who complete programs are two to four times less likely to re-offend than those who don't finish.

To make sense of these conflicting results, I turned to the work of two respected researchers, Dr. Etiony Aldarondo of the University of Miami and Dr. Jeffrey Edleson of the University of Minnesota. Both examined the existing studies to sort through the controversies and to see if some larger conclusions could be drawn.

Aldarondo and Edleson both conclude that the research does show that batterer intervention programs have an impact on *some* men's violent behavior. There is a "small to moderate decrease in recidivism among men who participate in programs compared to those who drop out or are placed in a control group, Edleson writes.[6] Edleson's findings reinforce the results published by Dr. Edward Gondolf, professor at Indiana University of Pennsylvania, whose research is still considered the gold standard by many in the field.[7]

Funded by the Centers for Disease Control, Dr. Gondolf conducted one of the most comprehensive longitudinal quasi-experimental studies of batterer intervention programs, following 840 abusive men and their partners from four cities over seven years, from 1994 to 2001. The study found that for men who complete programs, the highest risk of re-offending occurs within fifteen months after the initial program intake interview. After thirty months, only 20 percent of program participants had re-assaulted a partner, and at forty-eight months, only 10 percent had done so. He reported that the longer time goes on, the risk of re-assault decreases. Gondolf's research is notable for the high rate of partner and ex-partner contact he was able to have.

Edleson writes that while it is still not yet clear what components of batterer intervention programs helped create these changes, it does appear that enhancing men's motivation is important. Gondolf and Edleson concluded that batterer intervention programs are most successful when paired with a consistent court response requiring probationary treatment or jail time. Coordinated community efforts that include protective orders, mandated arrest, quick assignment to batterer programs, and swift consequences for men who violate orders or drop out of programs provide the context where programs work best.

Yet there are many instances where even the best coordinated community interventions fail to help men change. Professor Aldarondo's work explores how men with "weak social and intimate bonds" are at more risk for failure. He cites studies of attrition that show that men who complete batterer programs are "more likely than program dropouts to be employed, married, have children and be more educated. Program completers are more likely than dropouts to perceive the program as important and to admit their violence at their intake interview."[8]

Dr. Aldarondo concludes that "the higher the stakes are for men to conform to nonviolent social norms, the more likely they are to comply with intervention programs and to remain nonviolent following the interventions." He writes that this same dynamic impacts men who have been arrested or served with restraining orders. Men on the fringes of society, who are economically marginalized and engage in more criminal behavior, are the least likely to be impacted by either arrest or batterer intervention. This has significant implications for victim safety, especially when there have been high risk indicators like violent assault, homicidal or suicidal threats, or violence done in the presence of children. For abusers who are both on the fringes of society and who have engaged in high risk behavior, the only effective intervention may be incarceration.

Aldarondo argues that more needs to be done to reach out to the populations of abusive men most at risk. He also suggests that because of mistrust of the criminal justice system among communities of color, there needs to be active involvement by alternative civic and community institutions—businesses, non-profit organizations, higher education, faith communities, social network, and families—in an authentic coordinated community response to domestic violence.

Programs Are Not a Magic Cure

Batterer intervention programs are not always the best option for violent men. Sometimes incarceration is the only way to stop a man's violence. Some abusers are dangerous and need to be jailed before they further harm or kill their partners. But for abusive men who don't go to jail, education and violence intervention programs are essential. Far too often they receive neither.

I believe batterer intervention groups are still society's best evolving option for learning to be nonviolent. In a group, a man who's been abusive is exposed to other men with the same problems. Week after week he is held accountable, required to examine all the ways he's been abusive and controlling, and shown alternatives to violence. Though some men may have been able to make changes in individual treatment, a group is often the best place to break through the denial and rationalizations that keep abuse going.

The bottom line? Men acting abusively rarely change in isolation. Breaking the silence, taking responsibility, and being challenged by others is critical.

Some Men Change, Many Don't

It's been twenty years since my interview with Scott and Nancy and since Phil's suicide. In that time I have worked with hundreds of men. I would like to be able to write that I've seen many abusers change, but that would not be true. Close to 50 percent of the men who began attending our program dropped out or were terminated. Many who completed the required forty weeks may have stopped their physical abuse, but often remained emotionally abusive and controlling.

Sometimes men who attended our program appeared to be doing well but the truth was quite different. Some men learn how to "talk the talk" but never "walk the talk." I was fooled more than a few times by men who seemed remorseful and reflective in their groups, only to discover through contact with their partners that their behavior at home had changed very little. Studies have shown that men consistently report much more positive behaviors at home than their partners do. For some, their participation in a program is nothing more than another act of manipulation—faking accountability to get them through the program and off of probation. This is why ongoing contact with wives and partners is critical to realistically assess if there has been any change.

One warm evening in May, our group was discussing the effects of abuse on partners and children. A couple of the men took the lead—talking about the damage they had inflicted in their relationships. Others listened intently, slowly acknowledging their own legacies of damage. A couple of guys sat with arms folded across their chests, stony expressions suggesting they still considered their partners to be at fault. It's not an atypical mix: some men go deep, some put their feet in the water, and some stand back from the shore, refusing to budge.

Usually after six months in the program, I could identify the men who were taking the work seriously. They were the ones who were able to successfully defuse many potentially abusive situations. They had become more insightful about what drives their behavior. They were starting to report positive changes in their relationships as they turned away from abuse and control. While these men still had some distance to go, they were clearly on the path. When their forty week program had ended, a few chose to continue their work in our follow-up group.

I am disappointed more men don't make the same commitment. Their failure to keep working on themselves led me to wonder: *Why do some men change while others stay caught in an endless cycle of denial, minimizing, and blame?* Part of my motivation for writing this book was to see if I could get closer to an answer. The stories in *Unclenching Our Fists* provide some clues.

Individual Stories in a Larger Social Context

The stories that follow, because they are first-person accounts from individual men, may give the impression that the solution to domestic violence is solely a matter of individual change. It is not. Abusive men who've changed represent just one thread in the larger effort to end domestic violence. Though their personal successes are meaningful, action is needed on multiple fronts. Domestic abuse must be seen as a crime. Victims need to be protected; abusers need to be held accountable; and law enforcement and the judicial system need to become more responsive. Communities everywhere must take the stand that there will be zero tolerance for intimate partner and family violence. We must work to prevent domestic violence by educating adults and children, the next generation, about changing gender roles, healthy relationships, and nonviolent ways to resolve conflicts. Finally, many of the social conditions that foster domestic violence—poverty, economic inequality, and racism must be addressed.

This kind of large-scale social change may take generations, but in the meantime, change is possible for some families if men do the work to end their abuse. In our generation, there are some men who are doing just that. It is my hope that their stories can be helpful to victims and abusers alike, by offering a clear picture of the journey to nonviolence.

The Men's Stories:
Author's Note

The men whose stories appear in this book have agreed to have their real names published, with the exceptions of "James," "Michael," and "John." All other personal names, of partners, ex-partners, and children, are pseudonyms unless otherwise noted.

Several notes of caution to the reader: Some of the stories contain graphic details of abuse and violence. Though shared in the context of each man's process of accountability and transformation, they can still be difficult and upsetting to read. The stories should not be read without the context provided by the other chapters, particularly Chapter 3, "When the Man You Love Is Abusive." For women who are experiencing abuse in their relationships, this chapter will help them assess whether their partners are serious about change. Chapter 4, "The Last Word: Voices of Survivors," provides a forum for women who have suffered abuse to react to these stories.

-

Chuck Switzer

Chuck was born in 1943 and lives in a suburb of St. Paul, Minnesota, with his wife of forty-eight years, M'liss (her real name). He is a retired Postal Service worker and a Vietnam War veteran. For the first nineteen years of their marriage, Chuck was physically violent and emotionally abusive to M'Liss. After a particularly violent episode, Chuck was charged with domestic assault and mandated to a batterer intervention program. After becoming abuse-free, Chuck went on to facilitate groups for other men. He and M'Liss speak publicly and have appeared on Oprah *and* The Phil Donahue Show *to talk about the transformation of their abusive marriage.*

I was born in 1943 in Leadville, Colorado, the oldest of four children. My mother was seventeen when she gave birth to me; my dad was nineteen. They were very unhappily married. I think they only got married because they got pregnant with me. My mother was a housekeeper, my dad first worked in the mines, then we moved to Nebraska, and my dad became a farmer. We had dairy cows, wheat, and corn.

The four of us kids—two sisters, a brother, and me—were all born in less than four years. It was a lot for my parents to deal with. As far back as when I was three years old, I can remember my parents fighting. They would have these all-out brawls, fists flying, rolling in the dirt, my mom fighting just as much as my dad. Both of them ending up with injuries: bruises, black eyes, scratches—no broken bones though. My siblings and I were terrorized by them as well. My dad was the one who was more emotionally abusive; my mom was more physically abusive.

On the farm, we kids would shell corn and milk cows. I remember that whenever I was working around my dad, he'd want me to go away. He always wanted to be left alone. If I got to be too much of a nuisance, he would lock me in the corn crib and just leave me there. When you lock a corn crib, the lock of course is on the outside. So I couldn't get out. He'd keep me in there until he got done with whatever he was doing—sometimes that could be half a day. I was four years old the first time he locked me in the crib. I remember just sitting in there and crying.

My mom would haul off at random and beat the living daylights out of me, for any little thing. If she put the wrong thing in the recipe, stepped on an onion, if the milk machine fell off a cow—I was her main target. Because they had to get married due to the pregnancy, I think they both took things out on me.

We moved from Nebraska to southern Missouri near the Oklahoma/Arkansas border. We had a farm there, with dairy cows, row crops, and field crops. My dad was a philanderer. It seems like I knew more about his affairs than my mother did. I would hear about it from my friends, neighbors, and other relatives.

As I was growing up, I really liked to be by myself, to be left alone. I had developed uncontrollable anger. I was not a brawler—though I did fight with kids at school. I was a bully. If anyone challenged me, I would beat the living daylights out of them—starting in second grade, going all the way through school.

Religion became an important part of my life. We belonged to a fundamentalist church. The only time I ever got any peace was when I went to church on Sunday. I really looked forward to it. When I got there, I usually sat alone. The older people there were kind, gentle, nurturing. It was my one refuge from all the abuse in my family, for two hours each Sunday. I remember that time with cherished thoughts.

I didn't date girls much as a teenager. I had one girlfriend in high school—and I was verbally and emotionally abusive with her. Mom and Dad's abuse continued until I left home at age eighteen. When I went to college, I thought I would go into the ministry. I went to the Minnesota Bible College. My girlfriend ended up going to the same college as me; shortly after we arrived, she left me to be with someone else. Then I met M'Liss. She got me on the fall. I was attracted to her the first time I met her.

I wasn't really prepared for college. I realized that I was going to have to hire a tutor to catch up with stuff I never learned in high school. So I dropped out. My career goal of becoming a minister had to fall by the wayside. I went to work on the docks of Montgomery Ward. Then I joined the Marines; it was September of 1962. I was trained as an airplane mechanic. I served for fifty months, in Yuma, Arizona; Japan; and then Chu Lai, Vietnam. I saw combat, but, as an air crewman, I saw it from the air. To veterans, that's nothing. I wasn't on the front lines.

M'Liss and I actually got married when I was fresh out of boot camp. I was abusive to her from the very beginning of our marriage. The first time I physically abused M'Liss was on our honeymoon. We were both virgins and our first night together was a disaster. I thought it was her fault. I was so angry; I ended up beating her while I was on top of her.

After that night, I felt huge remorse and regret. I begged for forgiveness. I promised that it wouldn't happen again, the whole nine yards. All of that was bullshit—it was just a power and control thing I did whenever I thought I'd have to, to make sure she wouldn't leave the relationship. Violence was always my response when I got angry.

For the next nineteen years, I was physically violent at least once every month. And many more times emotionally, financially, sexually. I would throw whatever I had in my hands at her, like our kids' toys. I would throw them so hard when they hit her they would break. M'Liss had untold numbers of bruises to her face and torso. She wore glasses since childhood. I can't tell you how many times I broke her glasses.

I'd get angry about everything: If she didn't cook breakfast at 6:30 instead of 6:35. Or if she didn't park the car properly. If she asked me to do the dishes or sweep the floor, I did my best to screw it up so she wouldn't ask me again. I picked on her for the way she dressed, who she talked to, how much time she spent with her friends and what they talked about. I would tell her she wasn't raising the kids right. While I would criticize her childrearing, I wouldn't change a diaper or get involved in the ongoing care of the kids. I saw this as her responsibility.

M'Liss took care of the finances, but if I wanted something, she'd have to find a way to pay for it. And if she didn't, I'd beat her up for that. No matter what M'liss did, if she didn't do it the way I wanted, there'd be an incident. And of course I always blamed her for my anger.

All during this time that I was abusive, we were part of a fundamentalist church. The church didn't make room for people who had problems. So it was all kept secret. The fundamentalist church, in my opinion, just gives abusive men a place to hide.

Over time I became more and more violent. Sometimes I would put a belt around M'Liss's neck and drag her around on the floor. She ended up with rug burns from that. Once I pushed her through a glass window. Fortunately she didn't get hurt—though she could have been killed from the falling glass. And I was sexually abusive. There were many times I had intercourse with her where she told me afterward she felt raped. I had sex with her whether she wanted to or not. I also would do a lot of really cruel things: If she was listening to a tape player and not talking to me, I'd put the tape player on the floor and smash it with a hammer or with my foot.

The kids were all exposed to the abuse. If we were sitting at the dinner table and something set me off, I'd reach over and knock her out of her chair right in front of the kids. If we were in the car and she was giving me directions, but didn't give them to me soon enough or made a mistake, I'd beat her up while I was driving. The kids saw all of this.

The issue was never about M'Liss; it was about how I was feeling about myself. I was working for the postal service, which was a pretty horrible place to work. I had incredibly low self-worth and my job just reinforced all that. I felt lousy about myself and I took it all out on M'Liss.

M'Liss talked about us going to therapy. I tried it. At one point I saw a psychologist for PTSD for my experiences as a child. But back then, therapists didn't know much about the syndrome or how to deal with it.

The turning point came in 1981. We were at a party. I was angry about some things she said, and we got into a fight on the way home. I pulled the car over and beat her, punching her in the head. I hurt her really badly: her head was all swollen.

After we got home, without me knowing, she went to the police station. It was the first time she had gone to the police, although in the past, she had tried to call them during my violent incidents. I had always cut the phone line. A few times she would try to leave our home in the car, but I would disable the car so she couldn't go. She had tried many times to get away from me, but I always had been able to stop her.

But this time, she got to the police. Years later I learned she had decided that if I hit her again, she was going to the police. The police took her report and took pictures of her injuries. The city attorney filed charges against me for assault in the fifth degree.

The police never came to our house to arrest me. It was M'Liss who had to tell me that I was being charged. She asked a couple we knew to come to our house while she told me and gave me the papers. Our friends kept me separated from her. If they hadn't been there, I might have killed her. It was unbelievable to me that she had done this, beyond what I could comprehend.

I was scared. This was the first time in my entire life I'd ever had a run in with the authorities. I had always stayed far away from the police. It was the first time I had ever been held accountable by something more powerful than me. Once I was charged, I finally realized that what

I was doing was wrong. I didn't see how serious it was until I found out it was against the law. That was the wake-up call for me.

I cried and carried on for about two weeks. I went to see a lawyer. It became very clear to me that he could get me off, that he could get the charges dropped. But I decided right there in his office that that was not what I wanted. I knew that I was responsible, and I did not want to get off. So I went to court without a lawyer.

The judge agreed that if I signed up for a program I wouldn't go to jail. Otherwise, I would get a ninety day jail sentence and a permanent charge on my record. But if I completed the program and paid a $500 fine, the charge would eventually be deleted. I was put on probation for one year.

I started going to the group at the Domestic Abuse Project (DAP) in Minneapolis. I knew I needed to be in treatment, but at first I didn't like my group. I didn't think the program applied to me or my situation. I didn't really feel like I was benefitting. There was a lot of discussion about chemical dependency, which I couldn't relate to. I didn't connect to either therapist. I was also ten to fifteen years older than a lot of other people in the group.

M'Liss was going to a partner support group. We were still living together. Because I wasn't taking my program to heart, it was just a matter of time before I had another incident. I still had a gun in the house. I went in the bedroom and threatened to kill myself. That's when M'Liss got the restraining order.

I was brought before the judge and given an additional year of probation. I had to move out of the house. I had to surrender all my guns and continue with my program.

So now I was living on my own. I had to learn how to take care of myself, doing my own laundry and my own cooking. I started seeing an individual therapist once a week, plus joined a second group for men who are violent. I started really getting in touch with the true source of my anger. I knew, more than ever, that I wanted to get my family back together if I could.

Each week in my group, we had to report our incidents. We each had a turn to say what we did during the week. The rest of the group would give us feedback. I learned about "time outs" and other strategies to prevent violent behavior. I also became aware of my own feelings, which I had never done in my life. I was in the DAP Program for eighteen months, and in my other group for six years.

M'Liss kept the restraining order for six months. Then we reconciled and I moved back home. I knew we had to change everything in the marriage. We had to become more of a team.

There were so many things we did differently. We separated our money and made agreements about spending. Because I had a bigger income, I carried more of the expenses. I agreed to give her a portion of my income that would go into a joint savings. In order to take money out of that account, we had to both agree. I could no longer get what I wanted, whenever I wanted it.

I started sharing responsibilities around the home. I did housecleaning, dishwashing, a little bit of cooking. I also stopped controlling M'Liss. She was free to see who she wanted to, man or woman, anytime she wanted to see them. She could live her life, I could live mine, and we'd have our life together.

I had to always stay on top of myself. For me, taking a time out was my number one tool. If I felt my heart rate go up, or a certain pressure in my chest, my arms, or in the back of my throat, I knew I needed to withdraw from the situation. I could say to M'Liss, "Hey let's change the subject," or "Let's take a break."

Continuing to work on myself and getting support has been the key. I knew I needed to stay connected to the work of batterer's intervention. Most perpetrators don't want to do that—they want to believe that their abuse is all in their past. I don't think you can rehabilitate yourself if you don't stay engaged.

One huge thing that had to change was my attitude about women. Men throughout the world think of women and children as chattel, that women are merely here to serve. My dad treated my mother that way. He never conferred with her or valued her opinion. He never included her in any decision—like deciding to move to another state or build a different house, even which cows to get rid of. If they went on a vacation, my mother wouldn't even know where they were going when she got into the car. I treated M'Liss the same way. I had a major attitude adjustment to make, in terms of valuing women and seeing them as equals.

M'liss still has a lot of pain from all that I did. I don't think she feels afraid anymore, but she can be anxious, on the lookout for something stealthy I might do. She's pretty vigilant. It's still hard for her sometimes to involve me as her partner. I know I'm responsible for that. She still needs to talk to me about the past, to share some of the pain she has. As much as I may be remorseful, regretful, and apologetic, that pain is still pretty serious for her. I did that to her, and it's my responsibility to listen. I'm not going to say, "Well you've got to stop bringing that up or I'm out of here." I won't allow myself to do that.

We're going into our forty-eighth year of marriage and I listen to her whenever she needs to talk. Many abusers often cannot tolerate listening to the same stories, year after year. I do it because I'm responsible. It's my fault.

My eighty-five-year-old grandfather once told me he had no regrets. Quite frankly, I no longer believe him. I'm sixty-seven and I have a life full of regrets. I regret that I didn't stay in the Marine Corps or get a better education. I regret dearly that I didn't start out in marriage with a team effort—that I didn't understand how married life was supposed to be. I regret all the abuse and what that did to M'Liss. And my kids, who've been gravely affected. I don't think they made the best choices because of the example I gave them.

It would be so wonderful if a surgeon could just put a switch in our brain, throw the switch, and get our behavior to change. It doesn't work that way. It takes months, years, sometimes decades to change. I've been in and out of therapy for the last twenty-eight years. I've gone to therapy for my kids' divorces, my communication problems and control issues. I'm going to a therapist right now for issues of depression.

For a while I worked as a non-professional group leader with other men who are abusive. When they were just getting started I would tell them: You have to decide that you want to be a nonviolent person. Otherwise, you're wasting your time. You have to decide this is what you want to be and then you have to summon the physical and mental strength to do it.

M'Liss and I decided it was important to go public with our story. She's published a book. We've been on *Phil Donahue, Oprah*. It's something we do in the hope that we'll do somebody some good. The hope sometimes gets thin, though. People forget things quickly—so these TV appearances drift away more quickly.

We're not trying to save marriages. We're trying to help people understand that domestic violence is dangerous, that people get killed, that families get disrupted, tragically. We're trying to do our part to put an end to it.

Emiliano Diaz de Leon

Emiliano Diaz de Leon was born in 1976 and works as a Men's Engagement Specialist for the Texas Association Against Sexual Assault, in Austin, Texas. Emiliano and his wife Cynthia (her real name) are new parents. Their baby boy, Joaquin Navid Diaz de Leon, was born three weeks before our interview.

I grew up in Austin, Texas, in a barrio on the east side that was primarily Latino and African American. We were very poor. I'm the oldest of four—I have two brothers and one sister. We're all five years apart. My mother was a single mom, although there were men who came in and out of my life as stepfathers. But they weren't really supportive, didn't pay the bills. We lived on welfare until I was in my late teens; that's when my mom was able to get a job that paid a living wage.

There was a lot of poverty and drug abuse on the streets of my neighborhood. There was drug violence, domestic violence, and sexual violence. It was a bad neighborhood when I was growing up, and unfortunately, it still is.

For the first five years of my life, it was just me and my mom, living with my grandparents. They helped to raise me. Once we left that environment and my mom took up with my brother's father, we moved onto Fort Hood, the army base. I was happy that I had a new dad, but that didn't last very long. On the base, my mom was isolated from her family, and my stepdad was extremely controlling. He ended up being violent.

In fact, each of my sibling's biological fathers was abusive. They

were three different men, but they were pretty similar in terms of the things they would say and do. I think they were more violent to me because I wasn't their biological child. There was a daily dose of it. When my sister's father was living with us—that was the worst.

My stepfathers were all drug addicts. Drugs and alcohol were part of my home environment for years. There was violence happening in front of us, including brutal beatings. It was a daily ordeal, between waking up and going to sleep. I witnessed pretty much everything—it was incredibly scary. I felt powerless and hopeless about it all. I was so afraid for my mom's life, my life, and my siblings' lives. It was just a constant. I can't remember a time when I wasn't worried about my mother's safety—not only when I was at home but when I was at school or anywhere.

Even though my mom was going through all this, it never distracted her from her parenting. She never stopped taking care of our basic needs, making sure we did our homework, going to parent-teacher conferences. She worked as best as she could to keep us safe. It's amazing to me that she did what she did. Sometimes she would do it on the sly.

When we were the brunt of her partners' abuse, my mother would protect us with her body, so she ended up being the one who was hit and slapped. She would get really hurt and need to go to the hospital, but she never went. She never called the police either, out of fear for her life and the lives of her children. From the age of five all the way into my early twenties, she never reached out for help—not to a shelter or to a hospital.

My mom's life had been threatened by each of her partners. Each relationship ended with a brutal act of violence, often with a weapon. One of my stepfathers had pulled a knife to her neck—she thought he actually cut her throat. We kids would be the ones to call the police. When the police arrived, that was the end of those relationships.

With the four of us kids experiencing domestic violence and drug violence in our home, we had to figure out ways to survive all this. We each did different things. I tried to escape as much as I could. I would stay away from the house, go to school as early as I could. I got involved in Boy Scouts and a Catholic youth group. My mom wanted me to do this so I wouldn't join a gang.

My siblings and I were all affected differently. My younger brother has committed acts of violence and has been in and out of jail. My sister has been in prison for possession and distribution of drugs. My youngest brother is in a psychiatric treatment home.

I was fairly nonviolent, at least with my school mates. But the patterns started to creep in during high school, in my dating relationships. I wasn't sure how to be in a relationship, so I often ended up being angry and violent. I was behaving in ways that were very similar to what I saw in my family. I had no role models for healthy relationships, healthy sexuality, or healthy masculinity. I hadn't dealt with my anger, pain, or fear. I had never received any counseling.

I ended up with all the classic teen dating violence behaviors. I was intensely jealous, and when I felt threatened or insecure, I'd start yelling, pushing, shoving, and slapping. I stalked my partners, wanting to know what they were doing and who they were talking to. I had no remorse or concern about my behavior. When I was a sophomore in high school, I was dating this one particular girl. We were hanging out in a shopping center close to her apartment. She said something that angered me and started walking away from me. I followed her, pulled her, and slapped her — all because she walked away. I don't even remember what we were fighting about. She started crying. At that moment, I realized that I had seen this scene before — at home with my mother. I realized that I had a problem. I really liked her; I really wanted to be with this girl. But after I abused her, the relationship was over.

I knew I had a problem but I didn't know what to do. I didn't even know who to talk to. I went to my school counselor and told him what had happened and that I wanted to do something about it. The school had a program called "Expect Respect," and I was referred to that group. This is where I really began to do some important work on my own violent behavior and what I had experienced at home.

I had to face that I had been physically and emotionally abusive with girls. I had been treating them disrespectfully and sexually harassing them. It was the norm at home, the norm on the street. In my world, women were seen as property, as sexual objects. Men would harass women constantly, whistling, grabbing them, calling them *puta, bitch, whore.* I took a lot of cues from the street. Guys were always talking about their sexual conquests. There was no one saying it was wrong — everybody was in on it, including myself. In order to feel like I was part of the gang, the group, to feel I belonged, I had to participate. These were the only friendships I had, and I wanted to feel their respect.

The "Expect Respect" group met weekly while school was in session. I got to get out of class to attend. It was predominantly young men of color in the group. We had all grown up in the same neighborhood.

We were all living the same reality. We didn't tell people outside the group that we were attending the group; we kept it to ourselves.

In the group, we discussed anger, jealousy, healthy relationships, how to deal with feelings and anger management skills. I knew the issue wasn't all about anger and loss of control for me because sometimes I would do abusive things when I was completely calm. We talked about sexuality. No one had ever before had these conversations with me.

The groups were facilitated by a man and woman together. It was the first time I had seen a man and woman in equal partnership. It was really powerful to see them work together. It wasn't a romantic relationship. This had a big influence on me.

Even though I was attending group, I was still doing things that were emotionally and verbally abusive. I was never physically violent again but I would still call my partner names, interrogate her about who she was talking to, follow her around, check on her cell phone, ask her friends where she was going and what she was doing. I was also cheating on my partners, dating two women at the same time.

All the while I was going to my group, I was still hanging with the guys from the neighborhood. But it was getting harder and harder to be in both worlds. I was watching the men around me dying from drug abuse, from gang violence, dropping out of school, going to jail for domestic violence and sexual violence. I wanted to separate myself from that reality.

What that ultimately meant was that I had to make the choice to separate from my community. It was a difficult choice because my family and neighborhood were such central parts of my life. But I just couldn't be at home any more. As soon as I was old enough, I was out of the house. I knew that I had to do that if I was going to make any real lasting changes, if I was going to really live and breathe, that I ultimately had to get out. I still feel very torn about that.

I stayed in my group for three years. Each year our group had the opportunity to talk with a women's group who was also meeting and discussing these issues. Often these were women who had experienced violence, and they shared their pain and anger with us. My mother had never talked about her pain. I knew the violence was hurting her, but she didn't share it, so this was the first time I really witnessed women talking about the pain of being abused by men, and it had an enormous impact on me.

Another thing that helped was surrounding myself with different types of men. There have been several men who've been mentors to me. One man, Cisco Garcia, helped me transform my life and figure out what I needed to be doing. He was the model of the man I wanted to be. I met him when I was fifteen. Ever since then, I've chosen to surround myself with men who have made a real difference, mentors that embody the kind of manhood I wanted to be expressing. I had no idea what a healthy relationship looked like or how to be a healthy father. I think I was very fortunate that at such an early age, I got exposed to these other ideas about healthy masculinity.

After graduating from high school, I knew I wanted to work with the things I had experienced, as a survivor and as a perpetrator. I wanted to try to educate people about sexual and gender violence. It was my way of healing what had taken root in me.

I got a job at our parish as a youth minister. I met my wife Cynthia at the neighborhood community center; she was a volunteer there while she was in college. Cynthia is amazing: strong, brilliant, full of life, courageous, independent, with strong opinions. She came from a loving home. It's my first healthy relationship. We've been together for about thirteen years. There have been no incidents of violence or abuse.

Cynthia encouraged me to apply for a job as a children's advocate at a domestic violence shelter. I didn't think for one minute that they were going to hire me. But they did! I was the first man to have that job. It was amazing working with all women. This became the foundation for all the work I've done since. I've learned so much from Cynthia, from abuse survivors, and the other women in my life.

When Cynthia graduated from college, we moved to Harlingen, Texas, about five hours away, where she had a teaching job. I knew I wanted to be doing more work with men. So I started the Men's Resource Center of South Texas (MRC STX). We provided programming that encouraged men to heal from violence they perpetrated or experienced and to work to prevent men's violence in their community. After seven years of running the MRC STX in Harlingen, I got offered a job back here in Austin, working as a primary prevention specialist helping rape crisis centers around the state, doing sexual violence prevention work and working with boys and men.

I have spent many years thinking about how the violence affected everyone in my family. My mom is doing much better now. She is now in a healthy relationship with a man. But she remains cautious, protective. Years later, she's still healing. She realizes how much pain all that abuse has caused her children. She has to live with what has happened to all of us.

What is most difficult for me is how little I've been able to help my siblings. I saw my brother go to jail for domestic violence and my sister go to jail for drug possession and distribution.

I had to realize that I am powerless over their lives and the choices they've made. I've made different choices.

Sometimes people now have a difficult time believing me when I talk about the past. They have a hard time believing that I did those things to women. It's true that I was never arrested or charged or mandated to a program, but I'm not proud of what I did. It's part of who I am though, and what I needed to work through.

I've never had the chance to be accountable to any of the women I hurt. I wanted to, but they didn't want to talk to me. They didn't want to hear from me. My penance, to put it in my Catholic frame, is this: to take responsibility for not just my actions but for the actions of other men. I realize that my silence has made men's violence possible.

As a young man, I wish I had known that it was okay to be different than the men in my life, to act different, to talk different, and to walk different. I wish I had known that I would still be loved and accepted and wouldn't be hurt for being different. That's the kind of thing Cynthia and I want our son to know—that he is beautiful and he can be whoever he wants to be, can love who he loves. It's a message I never got. We talk a lot about how we want to raise Joaquin and the kind of people we surround him with, even the toys he plays with and the clothes he wears. We want him to be a different kind of boy, to grow up to be a different kind of man.

I'm at home as much as I can be with Joaquin. He has shifted all my priorities. I've been a community activist all these years, but now all I want is to be at home with him! Joaquin reminds me of what the possibilities can be.

"James L." (pseudonym)

James L. is professor of surgery from the Midwest. His patterns of abuse were primarily verbal and emotional. It was not until he was put under scrutiny at the hospital where he worked that he entered a program for abusive men. He has been in his group for eight years. In order to freely share his story, James requested that his identity be kept confidential.

I grew up in the 1960's in a big family—I had five brothers and sisters. My parents fought a lot. I witnessed a lot of shouting, verbal and psychological abuse, lots of anger and fury. There was some physical violence between my parents, though they wouldn't want to admit it. My siblings and I were expected to be seen and not heard. We were spanked on an almost daily basis. It was kind of the norm for the day it seems, lots of spanking, hitting, and corporal punishment, not to mention psychological abuse: the silent treatment, being roped into family arguments, a lot of "good guy/bad guy" stuff.

At the same time, I thought my family was kind of peaceful compared to other families I saw at school. It's hard to judge it through the lens of today. In those days, people thought abuse was only physical, that if people weren't being hit, then everything was just fine.

What I learned from my family was controlling behaviors: shouting, sarcasm, crazy-making, pulling rank. It all became part of my normal armament. I thought it was okay to be controlling and abusive. I thought this showed strength, because it got you what you wanted. It seemed to get you the grades. And that was important to me. I came from a very competitive family, and I was always trying to be as smart as my older brother. I thought this behavior would help me get ahead. I know now that it ruined a number of relationships for me, but I didn't see it that way at that time.

I went to an all-boys' school. I was frail and got bullied so I learned early on that you either bullied others or you got bullied. I learned that if I couldn't be physically powerful, I could be verbally and psychologically powerful. A lot of those "skills" were honed when I trained in the early 1980s to be a surgeon. It's awful to say but it's true. That environment is still there in surgery. But people don't put up with that anymore, especially nowadays.

I didn't start dating until I was twenty-five. I was working so hard in college that I didn't have time to date. I was like that character from the *Doonesbury* comic strip, the med student with perpetually dark circles under his eyes. I think I also learned in my family that dating was a bad thing. My siblings and I didn't get our drivers' licenses or have much of a social life. We were just encouraged to go to school and achieve academically. I know this sounds like a cliché, but if I got all A's and one B, I'd be asked what was wrong with me. I learned early on that this was a one-down world: someone is on top; someone is subordinate. We were trained to be competitive so I honed those skills, but at the same time, I didn't hone any emotional skills, even how to be a good friend. So by the time I became a physician, people my age were far more mature than I. They'd had relationships, purchased a car, bought a house, and had children. There was a lot of life I hadn't lived.

When I finally started dating, in medical school, I was really bad at it. I didn't treat women with respect. I thought a romantic relationship had to be stormy and controlling. I didn't understand that even if I was tired, women didn't want to be shouted at. I didn't understand that I could get empathy and sympathy from people if I just behaved myself. Instead I used a lot of shouting and scolding—just as my dad had done.

I went from one dating relationship to another. Relationships usually ended on a very sour note. If it was the wrong relationship, I didn't know how to get out gracefully. There are a lot of ex-girlfriends who I'm sure would never want to talk to me again. Growing up so sheltered emotionally, all the years in medicine didn't prepare me well for a healthy relationship.

I'm a very persistent person. Persistence can be a good thing when you're taking care of sick people, but it can be a bad thing emotionally. Whenever women began to reject me, I would have a hard time letting relationships go. I would start badgering the women I dated, even stalking them. I know I felt out of control when the other person ended the relationship. I would call the woman after we broke up, or would stay outside her house, pressuring her to reconcile.

I was thirty-four when I met my wife "Nancy." I knew from the outset she was wonderful. I wanted to do this one right, not repeat the mistakes of the past. We were in the honeymoon stage, but even when we were dating, I was already having some difficulties with my blaming and controlling behaviors. As soon as we got married, things got physical for the first time. On our honeymoon I grabbed her, leaving bruises on her arm.

I often got angry, lashing out when I didn't get my way. I assumed that I always had to be right. I got psychologically controlling, using sarcasm, withholding, badgering. Although Nancy could hold her own in the arguments, I always felt like the victim. It was because I wasn't getting my way. At the same time, I could also be supportive and encouraging, telling her she was smart, that she could go back to school. I would go back and forth between being loving and encouraging and controlling and angry.

Early in the relationship, we were diagnosed with infertility. We tried everything to get pregnant, including multiple in vitro fertilizations. We spent an immense amount of money because insurance didn't cover the procedures. I thought that gave me permission to become more financially controlling and abusive. It was difficult, and I blamed her a lot, telling her it was all her fault. The irony is that when we eventually got tested, the infertility turned out to be my problem, not hers.

When I was angry, I destroyed stuff, breaking things, even getting physical at times. I would hit, she would hit back, but I would always win. I'm ashamed to look back at it. Nancy had grown up with an abusive father. She started challenging me about my behavior. She would say, "You think you're a good person, but you're not—because you're not behaving like one."

I would behave just as abusively at work. I was treating people as if they were robots, as if they didn't have feelings—that they were just in the way. All the time, I thought I was being a good person. I thought that because I was taking care of the sick, my behavior could be excused. I would be so abusive to people beneath me at the hospital, to the night time staff, the blood bank, the lab staff. I thought I was justified because I was taking care of sick people. It never occurred to me that I could use a different skill set to accomplish the same thing and come out with respect, rather than looking like a jackass.

I was also having problems in the academic environment where I teach. I was not succeeding there. My behavior was detrimental to myself and other people. I blamed my problems on everyone else. Eventually, I locked horns with a very powerful figure in American surgery who was my boss at the time. He was reaching the end of his career and decided to focus on "impaired" physicians. Often, that means physicians with substance abuse problems. We didn't really have any of those in our department, so he focused on me.

He put out the word that if I did anything inappropriate, even to the janitor, he wanted to hear about it right away. He wanted to prove he was a tough guy who was going after abusive physicians to make them accountable. He was not my ally. He was out to advance his career, and he wanted to make inroads. The irony is that he helped me. He got me to take a hard look at my behavior.

Nancy and I had started pursuing adoption, and we planned to adopt a girl from China. Right when we were climbing on a plane to go get our adopted daughter in China, I found out that I had been denied tenure.

I'm a good physician and a good surgeon. And here I was, having my promotion blocked. I ended up appearing before a physicians' committee—a group at the hospital who hear grievances about staff who are in trouble. The committee decided I should go to an abuse intervention program for six months. I entered the program around the time we were working on the second adoption. In fact, one of the conditions Nancy set was that I needed to be in a program; otherwise, she wouldn't go through with the second adoption.

That hospital committee was the only authority that could have mandated me to a program. I never did anything that would have gotten me arrested; I was very careful about that. So I felt victimized when I started the program. There were lots of court mandated men in it. My first group felt very intimidating because most of the men had been arrested. I still didn't understand that I also could have been arrested as well. At the time I was only the physician. The whole thing felt like the movie *The Shawshank Redemption.* I was convinced I didn't belong in the group. I went up to the group leader and told him that. He said, "Just stay. Give it another few weeks. If it doesn't work, we'll call the university and let them know it's not working." So I did stay. I decided I would give the group six months.

The more I stayed, the more I realized that these men were not so different from me. I could have been court mandated like them. Although I was there to satisfy the committee and get that other doctor off my back, the truth was I needed to be there. I think I'd been waiting decades for someone to hold me accountable, to help me deal with this behavior.

I was a devout Catholic, and I was finding my behavior more and more shaming. I was raised to believe that if you were a good Catholic, you couldn't do bad things. Yet I knew I wasn't treating people in a Christ-like way. I was treating them poorly. Whether you're a Hindu or a Catholic or a snake handler, you either practice a moral code or you don't. I realized it doesn't matter what you do when you go to church on Sunday if you're not practicing outside the walls.

I began to realize some very simple things I hadn't before. I knew I needed to just stop my bad behavior. I had to start with the basics and tell myself that I could no longer hit, could no longer yell. I had to do what every five year-old basically knows—that when you're feeling escalated, take a time out. I learned just how abusive I really had been. I looked at a list of abusive behaviors and realized that I could check off many things on that list. I would sometimes tell stories in my group that would make people cringe.

I began to do really simple things. My leader warned me in the beginning, that because people were so used to my abusive behavior, I couldn't expect "attaboys" right off the bat. My wife did notice that I was beginning to change—to be less controlling and more collaborative.

One of the important things I learned came from Patricia Evans' book, *The Verbally Abusive Relationship.*[9] She writes about Reality One vs. Reality Two. In Reality One, somebody was up, somebody was down. Someone is wrong. Someone is right. But in Reality Two, it's different. Here we know there are truths with a small "t" and many shades of gray.

I realized I thought I always had to win. I had to react to everything with the best put down, the nastiest quip. I had the shortest fuse. I was the irate angry person who had power, and "irate" and "angry" is where I thought my power came from. I wanted to be the victor, so I gave myself permission to do lots of nasty things. To break this pattern, I had to tell myself that I didn't have permission to do those things anymore.

My six months in the group ended but there was no way I was leaving. I had made some baby steps but there was so much more to do. I was really connected to my group now. I realized it didn't matter whether we were court mandated or not, we all had the same work we needed to do. We all had to be accountable.

I began to do really difficult repair work with the people I'd been abusive to—making apologies, amends. Whether it was shopkeepers, police officers, or hospital staff, I would discuss it with my group and then seek out people I had been abusive to. When I entered the program, I had a universal reputation among the surgical residents as a real asshole, a real jerk. People began to notice that I was changing.

After I was able to get my more blatantly abusive behavior under control—the put-downs, constant sarcasm and cutting remarks, I started journaling to work on some of my more subtle abusive behaviors. The ways I wouldn't acknowledge people, not remember their names, turning around without acknowledging them. One of the reasons I stayed in the group is that the work goes on. That's one of the sadder things to accept—that it's a lifetime's work to realize how I was, how I am, to make amends—and to try to help other men.

The work in my group is about reinventing the foundation of the way you see the world, which is totally different from how we men are raised and the male privilege we are given.

I've been in my group for eight years now—every Thursday night. Nancy's been really supportive; she doesn't want me to pass this on to the kids. It's a tough group. You have to really want to be there. You have to really want to change and to listen to what is hard to hear. It's hard to be in the hot seat when it's your week to get called to the carpet on something. Our group is not a support group. It is a place to be held accountable. It was the first place in my life where I was held accountable.

I realized that this kind of repair work is an opportunity for intimacy. It's not anything to be ashamed about. I had been feeling awful about myself for a long time before I started the group. Ironically, it was almost joyful to finally get going in the group—to realize that this was the way you go about becoming nonabusive. I was almost enjoying the opportunity to go back and make amends. It was a relief and healing for me.

I've seen a lot of men come and go in the program. I remember one guy who came through the group many years ago. We were using Daniel Sonkin's book, *Learning to Live Without Violence.* At the end of the six months, he stood up in group and asked if anyone wanted to buy his textbook. He thought he was all done with this work. It was really a sad moment.

We just got a new guy in our group. He's twenty-two. A lot of us actually feel envious of him, that he gets to change his behavior this early in his life. He is in a relationship that's not going well. How many relationships did I mess up before I found someone who was willing to stick with me while I did my repair work? I wish I had known as a young man that there were other ways to handle things.

Here's what I would say to men who are just starting to work on themselves: Check your ego and your ability to argue at the door. Come in humble and be willing to take baby steps. So many men struggle and fail because they rationalize their violence to the point where they're never going to grow. To have real success, there is one thing to do—be accountable. It's painful, but you need to stick it out.

I don't pretend to be a successful graduate of anything. I realize I'm talking a good game here, but I know that I'm still a work in progress. Eventually, I'd like to get my Thursday nights back, but I'm not ready to leave the group yet.

I was finally promoted to full professor. I was starting to reach my goals, but the most important goal was to have my wife be proud of me and my children not be afraid of me. I was sent to the program for my career, but I stayed in for my marriage, for my family, and for myself.

Postscript from James:

It has been three years since this interview; I have now been in my group for eleven years. I have had many relapse periods in that time, slipping back into old, abusive behaviors. I've worked on identifying the things that put me at risk for this, how to catch myself early, and the things I can do to start "working the program" again. The weekly meetings and the continued presence of the group have been essential in helping me.

In the initial interview for this book, I said that my group was an accountability group, not a support group. Actually, of course, it is both; we all support each other in remaining accountable and working our programs, especially when we are relapsing into older behaviors.

As time passes, all of us in the group have been working on more subtle controlling behaviors. This work is harder because it involves behaviors which are less obvious, more complex, and trickier to deal with. While I dealt with the more egregious and destructive forms of abuse I was doing (physical, property, verbal) with relatively simpler techniques (time outs, not giving myself permission), more subtle abuse requires changing my basic beliefs about the world.

Instead of viewing the world from a power-over perspective, I choose to see it as a place where most people are your allies. I believe now that most things that happen may not be about me, and therefore should not be taken personally, even when it feels that way. I've learned that often I need more information before drawing conclusions. I'm also changing some basic concepts of self, going from a shame-based belief system (which can actually be used to justify abuse) to one in which I believe I am a good man who is flawed, occasionally does the wrong thing, but can do better. Working on more subtle abuse also means working on controlling behaviors we often don't think of (sexual, financial, psychological) and using techniques such as mindfulness that men are not typically taught.

In short, changing from living an abusive life to living one of respect is work that is collaborative and ongoing. It is work I will be doing for the rest of my life, but it is good work, and work I wish more men were doing.

"Michael" (pseudonym)

Michael was born in 1963 and lives in a small town near Provo, Utah. He works as a documentary film maker. He was married to his wife "Tina" for eleven years and was abusive throughout their marriage. They had six children, two boys and four girls. They were divorced in 2002. Michael made a film about the transformation to nonviolence, highlighting his story along with those of two other men. His ex-wife is an activist in the movement to end domestic violence and the author of several books.

I was the oldest of six children, three boys and three girls. My dad was a salesman for French's Mustard. Before I was born, my mom worked in the Mormon Church headquarters. We lived in Salt Lake, then a suburb, then, when I was eight, my grandpa's dairy farm. While we lived there, my dad started a retail clothing chain.

My mom and dad didn't really get along that great. My dad didn't really express a lot of feelings for other people. He was kind of a loner. He made a lot of big decisions without asking my mom—from moving out of Salt Lake to buying a car. It created a lot of tension at home. I think my mom felt insecure and had problems dealing with her own feelings, so in turn she was the one who was a little more abusive with us kids if we did something wrong.

She probably should have left my dad, so she could have a little sanity. But she didn't. She stayed and became semi-volatile. I was the recipient of her emotional frustrations. I was a mouthy kid and in my teenage years, I perfected it. My parents would give these little plaques to me—one of them showed a kid on a motorcycle with the motto, "Out of control" written on it. That was their description of me. I think I did have issues as a kid—I remember wishing I had a friend I could talk to about things, and I was angry about that.

My mom was the disciplinarian. Sometimes she would threaten me with "Wait until your Dad comes home." I did get into a big fight one time with my dad—he broke a chair over me, but that wasn't his usual "M.O." My mom would beat me with a brush, a broom—one time she broke her toe kicking me. But at the same time, she was my closest parent, the one I could talk to at the two in the morning. She was always there for me; she loved me to death. So I had this association that violence and love kind of worked together.

I was abusive toward my sisters. I remember one day when I was still in high school getting angry and yelling at everybody because things weren't going the way I wanted them to. I threw a rolled up newspaper at the sister I love the most and hurt her really badly. I would also try to intimidate my brother—threatening him with violence, acting bigger and tougher and smarter. My incidents weren't frequent, but I did have them.

I was looking forward to having a girlfriend or a wife someday—I wanted to have somebody. I had so many fantasies about relationships. I listened to all those love songs, all those Beatles songs. I passed up on some sweet girls in my life who were really good friends. I left it all to chance, to luck. I didn't know what the hell I was doing when it came to relationships. So when my relationships didn't turn out the way I thought they should be, I got violent and tried to shape them into something better.

When I was twenty-three, I spent some time fasting and praying that I'd find someone to be with. We do this in my faith. I did meet someone right at the end of this fasting period. I felt that God was so divinely involved with it that it had to work it out.

She wasn't really ready to get married; she had a lot of things she wanted to do. I was trying to control the relationship. I remember one fight when I threw my car keys so hard, they stuck in the wall. Another time I ran a red light intentionally, trying to scare her. What I did was totally inappropriate. She told her mom I was trying to kill her. Years later, I left her a message apologizing for that incident, but I never got to talk to her. She never wanted to talk to me.

After I graduated from college, I met a girl in Arizona. We started dating, she moved to Utah, and we got engaged. I had an incident where I kicked some furniture around. I never physically hurt her, but I'd push things around and break things. One time I intimidated her with a gun I had. She broke up with me.

In the Mormon culture, there's a lot of pressure to get married and start a family in your twenties. I had been looking forward to getting married; I was upset that it hadn't worked out. I was twenty-five. The older I got, the worse I got. I was not comfortable being by myself, ever. I was kind of depressed.

I met my wife Tina at a dance. We got married really fast. We met on February second and got married May twelfth. It was crazy. Part of what happens is that you abstain from sexual activity so there's a lot of pressure to get married. Parents are also afraid that we'll be sexual before marriage, so they rush us into it.

We had one serious argument during our courtship. I was up to my same old tricks. I was intimidating, non-negotiable, impatient, threatening. If I didn't like what she was saying or doing, I would keep us from going out.

I had these big expectations going into the marriage. I was already noticing that I still felt lonely, didn't feel I got enough TLC from her. I felt haunted that I had made a mistake, and I was afraid that she was a lot like my dad—reserved, not affectionate. She had her own mind and did a lot of things I didn't think were appropriate. So I would yell at her, swear at her, spit on her—calling her a bitch.

I did a lot of physical damage to the first place we lived, breaking pictures, tables. It wasn't even our stuff; it was just an apartment we were staying in for the summer. So here I was damaging and breaking other people's property. My wife decorated the house in a cute way and I would just go tearing stuff off the walls. She was in school, so her homework became a target for me. I always felt that her schoolwork was more important than I was. I would throw it everywhere. Another time when I was angry at her and she was out of the house, I took all her clothes off of her hangers and just threw them everywhere.

I was becoming more physically violent. We'd been married about five months. It was October and I had been deer hunting. She went to Idaho to visit her family. She came back on a Sunday, and I felt insulted that she had driven on the Sabbath. So I hit her. She had driven back that day because she missed me. We got into an argument, and I slapped her really hard and cut her lip. It was horrible; it still feels horrible.

One time after a fight she took off. I went driving and looking for her. I found her and somehow persuaded her to get into the car. Once she was in the car, though, I started yelling and swearing, calling her every bad name there was.

This went on forever. I had started making a lot of money in business, so we started moving around. Every house we moved into, I would damage it somehow. We lived in an apartment, a trailer, and two houses. I went through a sheetrock wall in each one. The house I'm living in now is the first I haven't damaged.

I would destroy her property, throw books around, pull her hair, spit on her, kick in doors, call her a bitch. It was ugly. I felt like I had married the wrong person, and I was taking it out on her.

I knew this wasn't the right way to be. What I hoped was she would see me having this violent behavior, understand I was frustrated, and do something to fix it. I wanted her to give me some TLC. I wanted her to say, "Michael, I see you're upset." But that's not what happened. I ended up scaring her.

My violence went on for eleven years. I hit Tina mostly in the first years of our marriage, but I kept throwing and breaking things throughout the marriage. I continued to threaten her with violence, however. I would charge at her and pretend that I was going to hit her. That was just as effective.

On December 7, 2001, she told me she leaving with the kids. I got really angry. I stormed out, and on my way out I kicked a picture holder with all our family photos. Some of our kids were watching.

I stayed with my mom for a while, then came back home. I was trying hard to be different, but I didn't have any skills. Things escalated and Tina once again said she was going to leave me. I got angry and had another incident. That's when she got a protective order—it was the end of January 2002.

A victim's advocate got involved with my wife. She was there primarily to support her, but she also met with me. She was really in my face about my violence. She told me about a program that works with men who have abuse issues. I didn't know that these kinds of resources existed. I signed up the very day she told me about it. When I walked into their office, I felt this incredible feeling, which in my faith is the Holy Ghost, telling me that this was the right place to be at the right time.

I really bonded with my first group therapist. I felt like he was my hope. I realized that everything I wanted, my entire family, was threatened by my behavior. I was really concerned. Can I really get better at this or will I always slip back into this behavior? Another group member told me that I could do it—that being nonviolent would eventually come naturally to me.

This is one of the first things I heard that made me feel hopeful. There were all kinds of guys there dealing with this issue. That really helped. I didn't feel as alone. The group was powerful. Everyone could see the honesty, or lack of it, in there. Only truth could really survive in that setting. It was sad to see some of the men, especially court ordered, just there doing their time.

The advocate that got me into the program eventually was put in charge of my visitation schedule with my kids. My youngest was two. I only got to see the kids one hour a week. That was hard. The advocate also helped me understand the physiological aspects of anger, the way the blood leaves your brain and goes into the muscles.

I tried to learn how to take "time outs." But I still felt like a "wussy" if I walked away from a fight. Or else I had to make a very dramatic exit. So I didn't take an effective time out for a long time, well into in the second year of my participation. For the longest time, I couldn't back down out of a fight.

I remember my first effective time out. I stayed calm, and said to my wife that we should talk about this later. I left the house calmly. After I left, though, I felt like crap. When I didn't just go automatically toward anger, I got in touch with all my grief instead. I finally had to accept the reality of the marriage. I felt really depressed. The time out wasn't what I expected, but it worked. I felt proud that I was able to do it. It was a turning point.

My wife and I separated for six months or so. Eventually I moved back in to the house. I felt really close to my kids, but things were very difficult in the marriage. There wasn't any more violence, but any frustration on my part was threatening. It made sense my wife would react this way; there had been so much violence in the past. She kept telling me, "I need to feel safe. I need to feel connected to you." I didn't know what to do with that as a guy.

I think I was honest with the other guys in the program about my abuse. I remember one night Tina brought a chart home that shows different forms of abuse. I could see what I had done. I wasn't going to pretend I wasn't abusive—I was. But after I had identified all the ways that I was abusive, I asked Tina. "What about you?" She got really mad at me.

She left the marriage for good in July of 2002. I guess it's better that we're not married, but I hate that our whole family is not together. I struggle with that. After the divorce, I stayed in the program. I stayed for two and a half years even though I knew the marriage wasn't going to be healed. I also worked with a therapist for a long time. I had a lot of things to think about.

What I learned was that abuse was a shortcut for me. It was a way for me to be lazy; it was a lot easier than working with my spouse to reach an agreement. Just like anything that's bad—abuse works. If you intimidate someone, you get your way.

At the same time, I know that for many years I tried to not be abusive—many years of what addicts called "white knuckling." But it didn't change anything—it was just stuffing my feelings. Eventually, something would just trip me out, and I would just explode. I wasn't really dealing with the feelings that were deep inside me.

It took me a long time to learn about feelings. So much of the time I would express anger when I was really feeling other things. In one of my group sessions, they handed out a list of thirty to forty feelings. I would have to look at the list sometimes to figure out what was going on for me. So much of the time, I just reacted. What was really going on was that I was scared. So it was important to figure this out.

I know I saw Tina as an enemy to me—like she was in the way of my happiness. I think there's part of me that still thinks she deserves some of the crap I threw out at her—although I know that's wrong thinking. I know that I was the first one to breach the trust in the relationship. It's hard to be empathetic; I know I still need to work on that. I don't think I can say I've been fully accountable yet. I don't know if Tina would think I've been accountable. For me, being accountable isn't about talking. My way of being accountable is to actually change my behavior. I haven't called her a name in over ten years. I pay all my child support every month. I have tried to change my patterns—so that my actions show progress, not what I say.

My film was about men who were trying to work on their own abusive behavior. I lived so much of my life without any knowledge of other ways to handle situations. Why did I have to grow up like this? This is why I wanted to make the film: I hoped perhaps it could help others a little bit. There are plenty of other guys who were raised in similar ways that can identify with this.

Recently, the prophet of our church was talking about how you should never get angry. I don't think this is actually the right way to say it. I think you should never act out of anger—but you're still going to feel angry once in a while. It's not a sin to feel that. This is where I think the Church makes mistakes some times.

In my faith, the leaders will say, "No man should ever abuse his wife or children." I would take that to heart—I'm a conscientious person. But I had no skills whatsoever. It seems absurd that you need to study to be able to get a driver's license but there are no requirements to prepare for marriage.

I remember the first time I prayed about this. I got on my knees, started with the Lord's Prayer, which was strange because it was not my typical way of praying. I expected God to chew me out. But all I could feel in my heart was love and understanding. That was a big point in my recovery because I did feel connected with and loved by God. It gave me so much power and courage to go forward. Without that, probably nothing would have ever happened.

It's hard to let go of old ways. You have to have a threat to something you love or want. I don't think if I hadn't been at risk of losing my family, I would have done this work.

I still need to stay on top of my patterns. I had an incident with my son not long ago. He's seventeen. We were driving to San Diego to pick up a car for him. He was giving me a little bit of attitude. I felt disrespected. This rage came up in me that I haven't felt in a long time. I was verbally abusive to him for ten minutes in the car—calling him a "f'in asshole." I flipped back into an old bad behavior. I haven't done anything like this in a long time.

So I pulled the car over and called his mother. I worked my butt off to figure out what went wrong. I've apologized to him. I've also had to examine what was really going on for me. He's young; he's got all his options ahead of him. He's charming; he has girls that like him. He hasn't screwed up his life yet. So there are some feelings of jealousy.

At some point you have to step back and say, "I've really screwed up." You have to say, "I haven't done this right yet, so there's got to be something wrong." I know that people can't change unless they want to. You also have to have people who believe that things can be different.

I was talking to a guy with abuse issues on the phone last night. I told him, "It's going to take time." It's okay that it takes time and it's okay to make mistakes along the way. It's like learning a foreign language. You stumble a lot at first. After a year, you're better, but you still don't know the nuances. Your wife may not want to hang in there with you. But at a certain point, it becomes about you and how you want your life to be. It doesn't matter what anyone else thinks anymore because it's all about how you want to be. This is the only place you have any power.

I feel a lot of guilt sometimes. Other people can condemn you real fast. I've learned that you have to be okay with other people loving you or rejecting you. You have to be okay with either of these. But you've got to be okay with your own self. That's where the power is, between you and God.

Robin Schauls

Robin was born in 1971 and is in his second marriage, living in a suburb of Minneapolis. He and his wife have been married for nine years. He has two step-sons, plus three sons from his first marriage. At the time of our interview there were four boys ages ten to fifteen, including his two nephews, living in the house full time. He jokes that "even the dogs are boys!" He works as a cardiac nurse. In his spare time, he coaches his children's sports: wrestling, baseball, and football.

I grew up in South Minneapolis. My mother is half-Mexican, my father Caucasian. I'm the oldest of three children, with two younger sisters. My parents are now divorced. They were married for twenty years. My dad still works in a factory as a janitor.

There was a lot of abuse in my family growing up. My father might be mad at me for saying this, but it's the truth. My father would just stuff all of his feelings. He would sit on the couch stewing, and then finally blow up. He was eventually convicted of second degree assault. After that, he moved out, and I didn't see him for a few years. As far as I can remember, there was always domestic abuse and drug and alcohol abuse by both my parents.

I can remember back to when I was five. I remember the tension in the house, lots of fights. I remember seeing small syringes in garbage cans. I never knew what they were for; now, of course, I do. When I was

a kid, I was taken out of my home several times to live with my grandparents while my parents were in rehab.

The most violent incidents involved both of my parents drinking. The kids got spanked, punched, our hair pulled. It went on until I was fourteen, when I was big enough to stop it. My mother was the one who would lose it on us the most. It got to the point where it didn't hurt at all. I would say things like, "Is that all you've got?" when she was hitting me. My mother also hurt my dad; he ended up with stitches. My dad abused her as well—he bit the tip of her finger off. I didn't see it, but my sister did.

I was doing terribly at school. I don't know how I even made it to high school. We had a lot of child protective workers involved in our family. They would tell me, "Robin, you're a smart kid." But I didn't believe them, because this was all that I knew. I never wanted to bring my friends home. I would leave the house at five in the morning and stay away until eight at night. But I was hanging out with the wrong people. Before too long, I ended up getting kicked out of high school.

In the midst of a lot of bad decisions, I made a few good ones. One was getting out of the house. But the bad part of that was leaving my sisters. I had been taking care of them. But I had to leave. So at the age of sixteen, I was living with friends.

When I was a little kid, I felt really scared a lot. But as I grew older, I got as tough as nails. I was very angry. I could just walk up to a kid I didn't know and if I thought he said something about me or looked at me funny, I would just punch him. Guys would tell me that I was a punk. I've had more fights with men than a professional boxer did.

I abused my first girlfriend at age fourteen. When she told me she was seeing someone else and didn't want to be with me anymore, I hit her. I felt bad about it. It was the first time I hit anyone in a relationship. But I was a bully. I was a five foot nothing, 105 pound nasty bully.

By the time I was seventeen, I had been in a string of relationships. My pattern was to have one girlfriend after another. That was how I would make myself feel better. I would tell a bunch of stories about who I was, get a girlfriend, and go out with her for a while. But when it all started to unravel, I became abusive.

When I turned seventeen, I met a girl and soon after moved in with her. It wasn't long before I became abusive. I was really jealous. I would push her. Then she got pregnant. I felt a lot of pressure to do something with myself. I lied about being a high school graduate and enlisted into the navy. She came to my boot camp graduation when she was about three months pregnant. She was feeling nauseous, but I pressured her into having sex with me. That's how I was. It was always "What are you going to do for me?"

While I was in the navy, I couldn't stand being away from her. I pretended I had an alcohol problem and got myself discharged. When I came home, I tried to fix things in my relationship. My girlfriend was upset, depressed, and didn't want to have sex with me. After our daughter was born, I had no idea what to do with a child. I was seventeen. All the frustrations, lack of coping skills, just got compounded when our child was born.

I joined the army reserve. When I was at my medic training, she broke things off. I know this happened because I was abusive to her.

I haven't seen my daughter since she was two. That's my doing, and I take responsibility for that. The pictures I have of her as a two year old are the last pictures I have of her. I talk to her uncle and her grandmother periodically. But never have I spoken with her or her mom. I did send her a letter a few years ago when she graduated from high school. I also included a letter to her mom, taking responsibility for my abuse. I'll never know for sure if they received or read my letters. If I could talk to my daughter, I'd want to tell her about my mistakes. I'd tell her that I know I wasn't there for her, that another man stepped in to be her dad and I hope he did a better job than I would have done. But I know I can't push a connection with my daughter — it would be disrespectful. If she wants to contact me, she knows how to reach me. It's part of the loss I have to accept because of my actions.

After my daughter's mother left me, the only thing I had going for me was my work. I stayed in the army and was stationed at Fort Sam Houston during the first Gulf War. My relationships with women were horrible. I continued to bully the women I dated, be jealous, and have unrealistic expectations.

I met "Jessie" when I was twenty. We got involved a couple weeks after we met and got engaged after about six months. We had a huge wedding and bought a house with her parents' help. I had been telling her lies to make myself look better. As she started to catch on and confront me, I became verbally abusive, yelling, raising my voice, intimidating her, and accusing her of digging in to my life.

Soon she got pregnant with our first son. Once again, I felt the pressure. There were lots of expectations. I didn't know how to do anything normal — how to manage finances or to take care of my responsibilities with my son. I was working nights, and I had started cheating on her. I was upset because she had a male friend that she was talking to. I thought, "That's not something you do when you're married." Never mind that *I* was cheating on her. Finally I had my first act of violence. We started fighting. . . . I ended calling her a bitch and hitting her.

Things got better for a while, and then she got pregnant again. We weren't expecting to have another child so quickly—our sons are only nine months, twenty-eight days apart. So we were under a tremendous amount of stress. As things kept deteriorating, I made everything *her* fault. The tension was escalating, I'd be emotionally and physically abusive, and then we'd cycle around into the honeymoon stage.

I would always say to Jessie, "If you wouldn't give me shit all the time, I wouldn't do this." I also would often blame my bad day at work or my finances for my actions. Then I would promise not do it again. I always felt inadequate, trapped, angry about her expectations, afraid that she would find somebody better than me.

Soon, our third son was born. Jessie was taking care of everything by herself. All the responsibilities of the family, parenting, and householding fell on her. I'd just go to work, come home, and fall asleep. If I had to take care of my sons, I'd get mad. I thought the kids were her job and that I was doing my part by working. If Jessie wanted to go out with her friends, I'd get mad and say "What about me? I'm the one working!" All that old fashioned macho stuff.

I continued to be jealous and suspicious. I started checking up on her. I'd check her phone. If someone called, I'd ask who it was. I'd meet her at work to see what she was doing. I was afraid she was doing what *I* was doing, because I was cheating on her again. Finally one night I came home from work unexpectedly. Her ex-boyfriend was visiting, hanging out in the kitchen. I gave him a look, and he got up to go. After he left, I had a huge violent incident. I freaked out. I punched Jessie, pulled her hair, and accused her of sleeping with him. It ended with her begging me to stop. I ran out of the house and didn't come back for a couple of days.

When I returned, I tried to smooth things over. But within three months, I had another violent incident that was just as bad. This time

Jessie called the police. My dad bailed me out of jail and gave me money for an attorney. Jessie ended up agreeing to drop the charges. We reconciled.

This went on for years, incidents followed by separations followed by reconciliations. I never took responsibility for any of it—it was always her fault. We ended up losing our house because I didn't take care of the payments. She moved back in with her parents. I was living with a friend for a while, and then decided to move in with her at her parents. Eventually, we ended up moving into a new place together. By this point, our boys were six, five, and three. I had another violent incident and moved out once again.

Jealousy continued to be my major issue. One particular day I kept calling her to check up on her. Then I came over to the house that night to see what she was doing. There was a babysitter there. I waited for a while; finally she pulled into her driveway with a male friend of hers. He was only a friend, but she had him with her because she knew I'd been escalating all day. I'm sure she was scared of me.

Her friend meets me in the driveway, yelling at me and telling me to leave. I said, "I'd like to see you make me." I ended up beating the crap out of him. I fought like an animal. He ended up with a broken tooth, bite marks on his chest, bruises, a black eye, and a fat lip. Jessie called the police while I was beating him, but I took off on foot before they got there. I used my military training to find a good place to hide. Then when I thought it was safe, I returned to the house to get my car. I was crawling so I wouldn't be seen, when suddenly I heard someone say, "One more move and you're dead." It was a police officer with a gun drawn and pointed at my head.

I was charged with assault and ended up in jail for the night. A friend bailed me out and then my dad came to get me. He thought that my problem was alcohol so he brought me to a substance abuse treatment center. It some ways it was a good place to be. I was in a program for veterans. It was a controlled environment and got me thinking about the ways I had been affected by my own family's substance abuse. But I thought I was better than everyone else. For me, this was just a strategy to deal with the court charges.

There was a counselor at the substance abuse treatment center who scared the crap out of me. He was a former Navy SEAL. I couldn't look at him because he saw right through me. He would say to me, "I bet you can be an abusive son of a bitch." I'd always been able to scam people and talk my way out of things, but I couldn't scam him.

I pled guilty to the domestic violence charges. I got sentenced to ten days in the workhouse and was told to finish my substance abuse program and go to batterer intervention. While I was in court, I got served with divorce papers. Here's how freaked out I was: just before I was supposed to come before the judge, I actually went to a pay phone and called Jessie to curse her out. So right there and then in court, I violated the order of protection and ended up with another criminal charge.

You would think by now I might have started taking responsibility, but I wasn't. I was still minimizing everything. I was hurt and angry about everything. I thought the answer was to fix my relationship. I still wasn't doing anything to work on myself.

When I got back to treatment, the group challenged me, "When are you going to get that you have a violence problem, that you're trying to control everyone around you?" I was upset—and couldn't understand why everyone in the group was ganging up on me. I almost left the program that night. The counselor brought me into his office and said, "If you don't stop getting hung up on this, you're never going to change anything. You'll end up in prison."

So I committed myself to not calling Jessie anymore. I had been so focused on trying to get her to understand me, to absolve and forgive me. I wanted to make her understand how I was feeling. Then I wouldn't have to do any work on myself. In my mind, it all came down to her. So restraining myself from calling her was one of the hardest things I had to do.

I finished my substance abuse treatment program and was going through the fifteen-week education program at DAP (Domestic Abuse Project) for my second time. But I was still thinking that what was wrong with me was an alcohol issue. I hadn't accepted that it was a violence issue. One day, Jessie asked me to come over to take care of the boys while she was at work. I had a protective order on me but things had been hard for her. I felt guilty for what I put her through. So I went over.

Unbelievably, the police showed up on another matter. They asked me who I was, and five minutes later, came back to arrest me for violating the protective order. I called Jessie and told her to get back home. She begged them not to arrest me, but they had a job to do. They were very courteous. They put the handcuffs on where my sons couldn't see them. My mother-in-law started arguing with them, and the officer got irritated. While he was stuffing me in the cruiser, he accidentally hit my head on the door frame. That set me off. I thought I had been cooperating. Now I was furious. I got angry with the police and started acting like a smartass. I ended up back in jail.

My mother-in-law had to put up $10,000 cash bail. When my counselor found out about my arrest, he confronted me. He said, "This is it. This is a felony! What's it going to take for you to get this? Are you ready to take responsibility?"

So when I went to court, I manned up and pled guilty. I got a very stiff sentence — sixty days in the workhouse, forty days of service after jail, five years of probation, and participation in a domestic abuse program. The judge told me if he ever saw me in his court room again, I'd be going to prison.

So I was now back at DAP for the third time. I had already done the fifteen-week group twice. Now I was back as the example of everything that can go wrong. We were a small group. We talked about our most violent incidents, our childhood. Every time we tried to blame our spouse, we were always brought back to our own responsibility. Even though I had heard this all before, I think I was finally ready to really hear it. It was my decisions, my behaviors, my not knowing how to communicate and take care of myself that got me where I was. I was finally ready to learn something.

I had only supervised visitation with my sons. I never realized how much they meant to me until I stopped seeing them. My ex-wife stopped covering for me if I didn't show up for our visits. One visit, my oldest boy confronted me about missing the previous visit. He said, "Hey Dad, where were you last week?" I realized the impact I was having on them. With my own dad being in and out of my life, I never had a consistent father. So I started valuing my visitation.

I started talking about things I had never talked about before. In the past, talking about any problems was a sign of weakness. But this changed when I was in my DAP group. The most difficult thing was telling my most violent incident. They told us to be detailed. The first time wasn't good enough. Neither was the second. Finally in the third telling, I really got it. I couldn't believe that I had ended up doing the exact same thing my parents had done. It freaking hurt. I cried like a baby. The person I swore I would never be was exactly the way I ended up. And I didn't have any excuses.

Once I hit my bottom, I kept talking with my group. My counselor told me, "You don't have to be that way. You don't have to be that person anymore. You're going to struggle; you're going to make mistakes. What matters is that you don't quit." I felt bad, but strangely, I also felt good. I had put so much energy, all these years, trying to avoid the truth about myself. I'd been trying all my life to make myself look good. It was liberating because I didn't have that darkness inside me. I could get it out there and talk to other men. I went to my group every week, and I looked forward to it. I stayed in the group for two years.

I had so much baggage. I had tons and tons of things I had done wrong and very few ideas about how to do things right. The group would help me to have better conversations with my ex-wife. The group pushed me to stop feeling attacked, to stop making accusations. The group helped me realize I needed to move out of my ex-wife's house. Our relationship wasn't there anymore. I was putting my energy into fixing the relationship, but I had already destroyed it.

What helped me to keep doing this work was my connection to the other men. I saw them struggling, just like I was, so I knew I wasn't alone. I had a probation officer with three hundred cases, but he still found time to come out and meet me for lunch with my employer. He believed in me. I know he didn't say that to everybody. He also told me that he was afraid I might mess things up. There also was my counselor from DAP. He never told me what I wanted to hear, but he always had the right thing to say. I also got support from a coworker. Once I started trying to do things different, things did start to get better.

I tried to have a new relationship, but it didn't work out. Then my probation officer made a radical suggestion. He said, "Robin, why don't you try being alone for a while? Just focus on yourself, your counseling, and see how it goes." So I didn't have a relationship for a couple of years.

Finally, I was discharged from probation. I still stay in touch with my probation officer.

After a couple years of being with no one, I met my second wife. We got married pretty quickly. Once we started to get serious, I told her about my past. That was pretty difficult to do. I didn't minimize it. I told her I was still working on it. She didn't run like hell.

In the first two years we were married, her son's father wasn't around. Then out of the blue, her ex came back into the picture. I thought I was going to be ready for this, but I wasn't. I had a hard time. I was really a jerk for six months. I knew I was having trouble, but I was having trouble stopping myself. I worked really hard to stay positive, but I had a hard time when she wanted to visit her ex in Green Bay. I was feeling uncertain about what was going to happen. I tried to control everything. I ragged on him; I argued; I was grumpy; I asked a lot of jealous questions.

My stepson got tired of hearing us argue. So he came up to me and said, "You always told me to speak my mind. So here it is. He's my father. And I want to know who he is." So my wife and stepson went to Green Bay. When they got back, my wife said, "I need to know that you're going to work on this. I'm not going to keep my kids away from their biological father. I love you. I've never given you indication that I'm going to do anything bad to you. I don't want to leave you, but this has got to stop."

I realized that these old behaviors are never totally gone, they can still hook me. Particularly jealousy, negative self-talk, self-esteem, those are the big ones. I have to watch myself, especially in the moments when I'm extremely tired or stressed. Several years ago, I lost it with my ex-wife, kicked the garbage can. That was a total slip. It was intimidating behavior. Now I catch myself, and if I'm upset, I tell her I'll email her. I notice my cues and do something different than the bad decisions of the past.

Negative self talk still is my huge thing. I work on this everywhere. I can still beat myself up too, calling myself a "dumb ass" when I'm having a hard time at school. I still have a hard time asking for help. So I have to talk to myself. I have to watch out for getting complacent or else I could lose everything I've worked for.

I think the fundamental reason I became abusive was because of how I felt about myself. I felt like a failure, like there was no way out. And then what I learned was that the way to deal with these feelings was to take it out on someone, to hit someone. And not let anyone be close to me. There's a lot of stuff I wish I had known as a young man. I wish I had known that the *Leave It to Beaver* family didn't exist. I wish I would have learned some communication skills rather than let things escalate into yelling. I wish I would have learned that it's okay to disagree and it's okay to be angry, but that it's important to step away when you're getting too angry.

I've learned a lot about how ideas of what it means to be a man affected my behavior and my thinking. When my father was at home, I never remember seeing my dad cry or us having quality talks. He was always saying f-this, f- that. Being accountable for your actions is the biggest thing I've learned about being a man. I realize now it takes more of a man to admit mistakes and ask for help, than just to pretend that everything's okay. I'm also learning what intimacy is. It's not just about sex.

I regret all the people I hurt . . . from the time I started beating people up. I've hurt a lot of people. I regret wasting a lot of my life doing the same thing over and over and over again. My ex-wife's still mad at me, and I don't blame her. I told her how much I regret what I did. I've asked her how it's affected her. She tells me she wishes I had been the way I am now. She's told me she's glad that I'm a better father though.

Everybody who I'm close to knows who I've been. And I want to talk about it. Hiding from things doesn't help. I tell people I used to abuse my wife, and that I used to abuse almost everybody in my life. It's hard. But going through all this and starting to help other people helps me. If I could have a conversation with men who are just starting to look at their own violence, I'd tell them, "Take the chance and go to the scariest place you're afraid of. It hurts, but once you get through that, you're going to be a stronger person for it. You have to confront all the crap that makes you do the things you do."

For me, it was confronting that self-hating voice. It was going to DAP, committing myself to the program, hitting bottom, and dealing with the consequences. And then having people who believed in me. It made such a difference.

All my life I knew how to make things worse. Now I'm learning how to make things better. I've committed to never physically harm another person, unless it's in absolute self-defense. I want my children to learn the skills I never got. Now I'm emerging as a leader in my family, which is kind of goofy. My younger sister has been in an abusive relationship. I've ended up intervening to help her.

When I look at the domestic violence homicide reports on DAP's website, I think about what could have happened if I hadn't gotten help. I want to be part of the solution, not the problem anymore. The pendulum in society is swinging. So I've been sharing my story publicly. I like doing small groups, roundtables. I agreed to speak at this national conference on batterer intervention. I've spoken at the university, saying that men who've stopped being violent are here. Contrary to what people might believe, you can recover from this—but it's a long process.

Going public is with my story is uncomfortable. The first time I did it, I felt like I was going to hurl. It was a domestic violence fundraiser about six months ago. But I told myself, I'm going to get myself through it. If I can help someone else, whether it's a victim or a perpetrator, that's what matters.

Steve Jefferson

At 6' 6" tall, Steve Jefferson is a towering figure. Born in 1950, he says he was abusive in all his intimate relationships until a near-fatal health crisis in 1991 prompted him to take an honest look at himself. In 1992, he enrolled in a batterer intervention program, Men Overcoming Violence, in Amherst, Massachusetts. Steve has three daughters, two from his current marriage and one from his first. A lecturer in sports management at the University of Massachusetts, he is also a certified batterer intervention counselor, facilitating a weekly group for abusive men in the very program he once attended.

I grew up in Newark, New Jersey, in a poor and happy home. There was no violence whatsoever. My parents were separated when I was three and my mother and I lived in my grandmother's house. I started spending time with my father when I was seven. It was during my second or

third vacation with my dad when I saw him pick up my stepmother and throw her into the fridge. She got a knife and went after him. This was scary—I never saw this in my grandmother's house. I never talked about it with my mother. No one ever talked about the violence in my father's home. It was the elephant sitting there in the middle of the room.

My mother died when I was eleven. She had remarried, so I lived with my stepdad for a while. My father pushed to have me. For two previous summers I had lived with him in Easton, Pennsylvania. These visits were pretty violence-free because he was gone a lot for work. I thought maybe it wouldn't be a bad idea to live with my dad in Easton. So at thirteen, I left Newark and moved in with my dad.

Things started to change then. It was a tough row to hoe. My dad was always on the road during the week. Things weren't good between me and my stepmother. She told me she was involved with my dad when I was born and that I had gotten in the way of their relationship. From her perspective, I could never do anything right. If I missed doing a chore, it would be, "Wait until your father gets home." When Dad would come home on weekends—there'd be punches and slaps. He was constantly drinking. My saving grace was my dad's stepfather. He would advocate for me. He would try to calm my dad down.

When I was fourteen going on fifteen, my dad attacked me with a baseball bat. I was playing a lot of basketball then and he knew how important sports were to me. He'd never been much of an athlete. He struck me in my right knee—I was in so much pain I couldn't walk. I still have pain from this injury today. My grandfather took me to the hospital. The police were called. They walked Dad around the block and told him he couldn't spend that night at home. Within two days he was back in the house. That just showed me that I wasn't safe—that home wasn't a safe place.

I kept playing sports. Basketball was my way out—even with my knee injury. I was not going to let that injury get in my way. I ended up as one of the top one hundred high school basketball players in the country. I got an award which my dad immediately ridiculed. He said, "I don't know how you got that award."

I would go home to my grandmother's in Newark for vacations. She said I could always come back to live. But I wanted to stay in Easton because there were better schools and better opportunities for me. I told her that I would tough it out. So I made a deal with the devil.

My junior year was the worst. One night I had forgotten to take care of the wood stove—I didn't bank it right. My dad grabbed a ladder from a bunk bed and broke it over my back. I went out on the roof because I knew he wouldn't go out there after me. I spent all night on that roof.

To stay away from him, I used to go down to the Delaware River for long walks or shoot baskets until two or three in the morning. The other thing that saved me was a job I got. My strategy was to stay out of the house so I worked a lot; I never came home for dinner.

In my senior year, my father was no longer working out of town. He was working right in Easton. Once when I was chopping wood, he said I didn't chop it fast enough. I had reached my limit with him — I had stuffed as much as I could stuff. I picked up a two-by-four. I looked at him and said, "You know what Dad, this might be the day that one of us dies. If you come at me now, the only one of us who's going to live through this is the one who wins because I'm done. I've had it." He looked at me. I think for the first time in his life he took me seriously because he walked away. He finally left me alone.

The rest of the senior year, from that moment on, it was like living in an armed camp. We hardly saw each other. This was the year of MLK's assassination, Bobby Kennedy's death. I was the president of the NAACP Youth Council. It was three months of hell. But I knew I had a college scholarship and I would soon be gone. He never laid a hand on me again.

When I got to Ryder College, I thought I had escaped. I was hoping all the violence was behind me. I met "Lillian" during my freshman year. We conceived our daughter "Sara" in the summer of 1969 — she was born in the spring of 1970. With the stresses of being a breadwinner on one hand and an athlete on the other hand, my own abuse began to emerge. When things got hard, I would often want to escape. Lillian would want to talk about it and tell me I needed to stay. She would plant herself in front of the door. This made me angrier.

I felt trapped economically. I had to turn over my checks to her — this reminded me of living with my father. I also didn't like the way she looked and I made comments about her appearance. I started having affairs with other women and I became more verbally abusive with Lillian. This went on for seven years.

The worst incident with Lillian happened during our second pregnancy. We had a fight. She stood in front of the door. I was so angry I hit her in the stomach. I didn't care. Later I took her to the medical center. Fortunately the baby was okay, but we later decided to have an abortion.

I think my emotional abuse of Lillian was the most damaging. I used to go for the jugular when I talked to her. I told her she was a fat pig. I used to say, "How can you expect me to be in this relationship with you looking like that? I'm not proud to go out in public with you." I told her this consistently. No matter what she did, it wasn't enough.

For many years during my marriage to Lillian, I had a girlfriend, "Janet." When I was twenty-seven, things with Lillian finally fell apart. I moved to Massachusetts to go to graduate school. Janet moved up with me. I was violent in this relationship as well.

Once I beat her up in the car on my way to the airport. I was starting to realize how much like my father I was. This scared me to death. I had vowed that I would never be like him. We went to couple's counseling with a priest I knew from high school but this didn't help me stop my violence.

Things with Janet fell apart. I started a new relationship with a woman named "Beth." She had talked to me about doing an inventory—looking at the patterns in my life. So I did this. I asked myself, "What is the one thing that's been consistent in my relationships with women?" And I realized that I had found wonderful women who had loved me, and I sabotaged every last one of those relationships. I realized I had a fear—when things were going well, this scared me to death. So when things were good, I would do everything in my power to go back to my old habits. I realized that I was going to be old and alone if I continued doing what I was doing. I would be sixty or seventy years old and all by myself.

My relationship with Beth fell apart. Then I met Leticia. She was a basketball player, and I was the coach of her team. She was one of the great loves of my life.

I had promised myself I would never hit another woman again. But one day we had a fight, and I hit her. I knew that I had slipped back. I knocked her down and told her she had to leave. I started thinking about killing myself. We were in the car, and I was driving about a hundred miles per hour and I thought, "I'm going to crash this car." Then I said out loud, "I'm not going to let anyone else have you." Fortunately, she talked me out of it. I never heard anybody talk so fast in their life. She got through to me.

I was more violent than ever before in my life. One Super Bowl day, Leticia was supposed to come over. She didn't show up. So I went out and stalked her. I had never done this before. I was scaring myself. Another time, I hit her while we were on the campus. The campus police witnessed it and suddenly three police cars pulled up. Leticia refused to press charges. By this point, we'd been together for four years. I was so in love with her and really afraid I was going to lose her. I didn't want to lose control. I had invested everything in my life in this one person. If she left me, I felt like I'd have no life left.

Our relationship was a complete rollercoaster. We came apart, we got back together. Once when we were separated, she came to my house to get her things when I wasn't there because she didn't know how I would react. Ultimately, we reconciled again. But she was scared of me. She felt that the best way she could be safe was to be with me. She was afraid if she left, she didn't know what I would do.

Everything finally came to a head when I was forty-one years old. Leticia had just broken up with me. Not long after I developed a rash on my arms. Then I turned maroon from the top of my head to the bottom of my feet. I had a 105.6° temperature. I drove myself to the university clinic. They called an ambulance and took me to the hospital. It turns out that I had Toxic Shock Syndrome.

I was put in a room in the basement next to the morgue because the hospital was full. Everybody who treated me came in with protective gear. They didn't know if I was going to live or die. I hallucinated for four days. During that time, I flashed on an article I had read about a program for batterers. I said to myself, "If I live through this, I'm going to put myself in that program."

I got out of the hospital and got the name of the program's director, a man named Steven. I called him for an intake, but I never made the appointment. I kept procrastinating. Steven kept calling and asking me about the intake. He called me every week until I finally got myself in there.

I had a lot of fear about going into the program. No guy wants to be seen as a batterer. No man worth his salt wants to be seen as someone who beats up on women. Although we know men do that, this has always been "behind closed doors" stuff. It's hard to make what was private now public and to know that you're going to be in a group with men who are all batterers. And I know that if I'm in that room, it means I'm one too. This was not something that I found easy to accept.

To be really honest about it, there was some crazy self-deception in my head. I was thinking, "If I do this program, maybe Leticia will stay." So the program was something I was doing to keep the relationship—it wasn't for me. The intake interview was really difficult. All those questions about my behaviors were all the things I least wanted to discuss, least wanted people to know about. I know I wasn't totally truthful during that intake. I wanted to put the best spin on my behavior I could. I wasn't in a place where I could be totally honest about my life. I couldn't own everything, but what I did own really scared me. As I looked at the power and control inventory, I could really see what kind of problem I had. There was no way I could sit there and say, "That's not me."

The first day of group, I measured myself against the other men. I told myself, "These guys are worse than me." I didn't want to see myself like them. I wanted to think I was different. I was still in denial. There were fourteen men in my group. It was a small room so it was very crowded. I kept my check-ins very short. It was me and thirteen white guys sitting in the room. As the weeks went on, guys started dropping out like flies. In the end, there were only five of us.

During one group, I had to talk about my "time out" with Leticia. But my time out was actually an abuse incident from the program's point of view. What happened was that Leticia changed her mind about being sexual with me. I told her I needed to take a time out, but instead of leaving for an hour so I could calm down, I spent twenty minutes spewing out all kinds of invectives. As I was doing this, I could see all the trust draining out of her eyes. As I was sharing this with my group, I realized all of the sudden that there was no chance left with her. And I knew I needed to be in my program for *me* . . . not to save my relationship.

One of the guys in the group was like a teacher's pet. He did a lot of the confronting of the other guys. It seemed like he had his shit together. He was getting ready to leave the program and was going to get married one week later. Well, he ended up having the marriage annulled—he'd had an incident at his wedding. He came back to the program. This really showed me that if I was going to do this well, I was going to have to dig really deep.

Learning about the cycle of violence had a huge impact on me. I saw myself clearly in that cycle. I could remember all the honeymoon gestures I had made—the flowers, the candy. I realized there was a cycle of violence in my relationship with my father. I remember sitting in the kitchen the night after he hit me—making excuses about what had happened.

I stayed in the MOVE program for about two years. I completed the basic program and was in a follow up group for about a year. I decided to approach Leticia, who was living in Minnesota, to see if she would meet with me. I wanted to be accountable to her for what I had done.

It was the middle of winter when I went to see her in Minnesota. I told her I wanted to hear from her about what it was like being with me. She agreed to meet with me in my motel room. She sat by the door. We talked for four hours. She told me how she still flinches whenever anybody raises a hand near her. She said she is always vigilant and doesn't feel as safe as she had before our relationship. She told me how hurt she was that someone who professed to love her could bring this into her life. And she wasn't sure if she could recover from it.

I finally understood just how afraid she had been. As the conversation deepened, she actually moved away from the door. We ended up hugging at the end of the talk. I think it was a gift for both of us. I'm not sure I deserved the gift—but she gave me a gift I appreciate.

I have a lot of regret about what I've done. To this day, Lillian (my ex-wife and mother of my first-born) is still very angry at me. We're always linked because of our daughter. The last conversation we had was when I got my doctorate. She wasn't going to let our daughter come to my graduation ceremony. I think she feels very betrayed by me and by my successes. She's had to struggle for a lot in her life as a single mom. Even though I did provide money, she needed more than that from me.

When Sara graduated from college, I tried to talk to Lillian—to have a passable conversation. But she didn't want to talk to me. I wrote her a letter — saying that if she ever wanted to sit down and talk about anything related to our marriage, I would do that. But she's never wanted to.

Truthfully, it's my daughter Sara who has borne much of the weight of my abusive behavior because no matter which woman I was with, Sara was always there. She would witness it all. I found out years later that she would go out for walks in the middle of the night; when she was twelve, thirteen years old, just to escape the fighting. I had no idea at the time.

She used to slip out into the middle of the night, just like I had with my father.

"John" (pseudonym)

John was born in 1960 and has been married to his wife, "Kate," for over thirty years. They have two sons. Kate works in the health care field. John is a contractor and has been self-employed for over thirty years.

We moved around a fair amount when I was growing up. My dad was a business man, and was very upwardly mobile. I was born in Pennsylvania, but we moved to Indiana, Ohio, New Jersey, and then back to southeastern Pennsylvania where I graduated from high school. There were four kids in my family, an older brother and sister, a younger sister, and me.

There was definitely abuse in my family. My father was economically and emotionally abusive toward my mother. I was singled out by him for physical abuse. He did some pretty horrible things to me between the ages of five and thirteen. I remember being hit with a belt for minor infractions by my dad when I was very young. He had a paddle that he would use sometimes, other times it was his belt or his hands.

I don't remember him ever hitting my sisters. I think he threw something at my brother once. The amount of abuse varied — sometimes we'd go months without an incident, sometimes it happened every week. He was a pretty angry, volatile person. Alcoholism had a lot to do with it, though I don't give him that as an excuse.

As kids, we were walking on eggshells all the time. I had to develop survival skills, especially learning how to read his cues. I had to learn, too, to fade in to the background and know when to get out of the house.

The last time he put his hands on me, I was thirteen. I was out with my friends and I was late getting home because we missed the train. I tried to explain but he didn't believe me. He thought I was lying. He got angry, grabbed me by my shoulders and smashed my head against a kitchen cabinet. I remember my mom screaming. I got knocked out. Next thing I knew, I was waking up on the floor.

My mom got me a bag of ice and had me sit down on the living room couch. I heard her telling my dad there was a lump the size of an egg on the back of my head, but he said that couldn't be. He came in to talk to me a few minutes later. He wouldn't say he was sorry, but he told me he loved me. Shortly after, my parents left—they had dinner reservations. I remember being mad at my mother for leaving with him. It took me a while to realize that she didn't have a choice but to go on as if everything was normal. I don't think at that time she could have told him she wasn't going to go.

I didn't date a lot until I met my wife, Kate. We met through a mutual friend. I was dating her friend, and when things fell apart in that relationship, Kate and I got together. I was eighteen and she was sixteen. A couple years later we were married.

We started having problems in the marriage after we'd been together about six years. It took me another ten years to realize I had a part in them. I think my problems existed long before I realized they did.

If I had a bad day, I'd come home and take it out on Kate. I'd start a fight about something that wasn't cleaned up or something else going on in the house. I'd be slamming doors and stomping around, throwing a fork from twenty feet away. I controlled her a lot through my anger. I was often pissed off about something, probably 70 percent of the time.

I was also very controlling. I felt like I should make the decisions about how money got spent. Take the phone bill, for instance. The phone was a lifeline for Kate. We lived in a rural area, and the phone was the way for Kate to stay connected to her friends and family. I would give her all kinds of grief and make all kinds of angry accusations about the amount of time she spent on the phone. I also controlled her by not spending money on her car. I didn't want her going out. Like when our son was born. She was afraid to drive because the tires were so bad. These were just some of the ways I tried to isolate her. With the phone, she couldn't talk to anybody; with the car, she couldn't go anywhere.

My behaviors were driven by my insecurity. I didn't want her having friends or meeting people. I felt afraid she was going to leave me, want somebody else. I was afraid that I wasn't good enough. So I didn't like her getting out into the world and meeting other people.

Our oldest son was born in 1994. We had a great stretch in our marriage when he was born. We were so happy and excited. But pretty soon this all shifted. Kate was realizing how completely her life had changed as a result of having our son. But my life hadn't changed much. I was pretty much still going on the way I had—with the same hobbies, doing whatever I wanted to do whenever I wanted to do it. I really wasn't involved in any of the second or third shifts of caring for our child. I remember our fighting got more intense and the cycle of my abuse got shorter and shorter. There was less of that honeymoon time before the next incident.

Our son witnessed a couple of our fights. I remember stomping out of the house while he was crying in his high chair.

I was an avid hunter, and I had a lot of guns. Kate was definitely intimidated by this. I had a den where I kept the guns. One time after we were fighting, I said, "I'm not going to take this anymore." I went stomping up to my den. She was afraid that I was going for my gun.

All along, I was thinking that my anger was *her* fault. That if only she would listen better, understand me better, be more reasonable, then these things wouldn't happen. We went to a marital therapist. He was pretty terrible. He put a couple of band aids on our problems. But it all resurfaced again. I think it's because I really believed it was 98 percent her fault.

I blamed Kate all the time, but she was also my only source of support. I didn't really have any friends, just drinking buddies. Drinking made my anger more intense. Kate also started to disappear, spending more time out of the house, going off to drink herself. It was her anger at me, coming out that way.

As a result of my abuse, Kate had an emotional breakdown. She got on long term disability. While she was on disability, I was emotionally abusive to her. I remember telling her that I didn't think she would ever get another job. I told her that she wasn't worth what they were paying her for disability. I would undermine her with our son, saying things to him like, "Your mom is having a bad day" after I would be the one to drive her nuts.

Kate started seeing a therapist who was getting trained at a batterer intervention program. This therapist was transitioning from traditional family therapy to the domestic abuse model of accountability and cultural context. Sue joined a women's group. She was getting increasingly enlightened about what she was living with—the power, control, and abuse.

We started to see her therapist for couple's therapy. I was getting really ticked off every time we went because according to the therapist, everything was my fault, which I didn't agree with. I really resisted the idea that I was actually responsible for what was going on. I didn't like that at all.

Eventually, the program opened a satellite nearer to our home. I reluctantly joined the men's group. It was Kate's idea. I said I would try it. Someone said something about the program being six weeks so I thought, "Okay, within six weeks I'll get everyone to see how unreasonable Kate is and then life will just go on." I didn't realize that six weeks was just the orientation phase.

I remember the first time I talked about an argument Kate and I had over the groceries. I thought she was being a jerk for confronting me for not helping. I felt she was being unreasonable. As I told the story, and people started asking me questions, I started to realize that no one was going to agree with me that she was unreasonable. Instead, they were challenging me about why I wasn't helping more.

There were about eight guys in my group. These groups usually have sponsors, men who are further along in their process of acknowledging their controlling behaviors. But this was a new group, so there were no sponsors yet to hold us accountable. It was very easy to get the other guys to collude with me. Basically, we were all in the same boat—none of us really wanted to be there.

I was really upset, confused, and very angry. I remember talking to some of the other men, saying, "I don't know what the heck the facilitators are talking about." Some the guys were wondering if this was some kind of cult. We thought the group leaders were nuts. They kept talking about power and control. We really wanted to talk about our relationships. They wanted to talk about the broader picture—about inequality. They would show us film clips, trying to get us to open our eyes to how power is constructed in our society by race and class and gender. Eventually I came to understand how power is based on race or sexual orientation. Okay, I thought, I could get that. But when they started talking about the gender piece, I couldn't agree with that.

Around the six week mark, the facilitator told me that Kate was coming in the following week to read a letter to me. I think they realized that Kate and I were at the breaking point in the relationship and something needed to happen. When the therapist told me that Kate was coming, I said, "You've gotta be kidding me. Nobody asked me." And she said, "Why should we have to ask you?" So then I said, "Nobody told me." The therapist replied, "Well, I'm telling you now." I flipped out. I was furious, and I stormed out of the group.

I called a couple of guys I knew would collude with me because they didn't want to be in the same boat. They backed me up—saying "Darn right you're mad." Then I called the therapist and said. "This is bullshit." I told her I wasn't coming to the next group. She said, "Well, that's up to you." So I asked if they were still going to read the letter and she said "Probably, I don't know; I'll figure it out." I told her there was no way I was going to come to the group, that I'd sooner put a gun in my mouth than show up and hear that letter.

I went home. I remember walking in the door. I told Kate I was upset, but not at her. I didn't process it with her. The program had called her before I came home to say that I was upset. So she must have been nervous.

All that week, I was falling apart, breaking down and crying. I was a total basket case. I think what was going on for me was the fear of losing control and the shame of having people know what I'd been doing; the feeling that I was going to be exposed.

There was one guy in our group who had been working on his issues longer. He had been at a group at the other program site. He was able to help me see a lot of things that I was doing. He talked me off the ledge. He said, "What are you so afraid of? You're not the first person to ever do this stuff. Lots of guys have done this." He talked about some of the things he had done that were the same as my abuse or even worse.

I realized that I needed to show up for the letter or else the relationship with Kate would be over. I decided to go to the group. But I had a safety net—if I got really ticked off, I would get up and leave.

Kate came in with a couple of the other women. She talked about the gun incident. I was shocked when I heard her say she thought I might kill her. I had talked about this incident with the group before, but of course I had minimized it. I told the group that I never would have shot her. But when Kate came to the group, I started to realize that what was important was what *she* felt and believed the night of the incident. From her experience, I was so angry and volatile that she was afraid I was going to shoot her.

Kate also talked about my control over the phone and car. She talked about the economic abuse and my use of pornography. She talked about what it was like living in a climate of fear. I sat and listened. Then, when she was done speaking, I owned it all—I acknowledged that I had done all those things. It was the first time I had taken responsibility with her.

I think what helped me own everything was the power of the group setting. You can deny your abuse one on one in your house, but you can't deny it in a room full of people. There were fifteen people there—the men in the group, a couple of women, a couple of other therapists, but it felt like two hundred.

I felt a lot of things that night. I felt really bad for Kate. I really hadn't gotten it until then what it was like to live with me. At the same time, I felt okay about the whole process. I got through it. I felt fifty pounds lighter. People were supportive; they weren't judgmental. I knew a lot of people there wanted to help me. When I left the group that night, I felt like a helium balloon. I wasn't trying to cover my butt or continue my illusions. I felt good. If you had asked me what I was going to feel like before I went in there, I never would have picked that feeling.

Now I wanted to know—what can I do to make things better? What should I do today, tomorrow, next week? The women gave me some ideas. The first thing was to get rid of the guns—I put them in a storage locker and gave the keys to one of the men in my group. I started working on second shift stuff—doing the laundry, a lot of domestic stuff I hadn't done. I got into recovery as well, to deal with my alcohol abuse. Things with Kate started to get better.

I realized how much my substance abuse impacted my domestic abuse. I was more volatile if I was drunk or high. I was less accountable when I was drinking. Because of my substance abuse, there was ongoing economic abuse. It's not just what I spent on drugs or booze, but all the days I couldn't get to work because of my addictions.

Our second son was born. It was so totally different than when my older son was little. Now I was a dad who was involved, a dad who was not angry all the time. If I did get angry, I was accountable for it. I was in recovery. I was totally involved in the second shift at home. By then I was PTA president at my older son's school. I was vastly different than the isolated, angry dad he had when he was younger.

Thinking about my socialization as a man was really important. I think I got the message growing up that men are superior—that we're supposed to make all the decisions and be the bread winners. That women had certain roles—raising the kids, taking care of the house, maybe working outside the house as long as they were home in time to get dinner on the table. I got the message from my dad and from the media that men should be in control.

I also learned early on that men don't typically rely on other men for emotional support. It's okay if you want to talk about the score of the game, or go hunting or fishing. But if want to say, "I'm really sad today," another man is not who you'd talk to. Men don't talk about emotional issues with other men because you'd be thought of as gay. It's the same reason why new men in the program don't pick up the phone to call their sponsors—because it's not seen as manly.

Not only did my relationship with Kate change, but my friendships have changed dramatically. I started to be able to have real relationships with other men—where we really know each other's stories. We plan outings with the kids; we plan dinners. We talk about things on a regular basis—our fears, our concerns. I realized that if I can't have that emotional closeness with men, I can't have it with Kate either. Before, my emotional safety net was just one strand—that put a lot of pressure on my relationship with Kate.

Kate and I are doing much better, but it hasn't been perfect. We've had our ups and down. As I changed my behavior, I thought I was doing such a great job that it made me less willing to hear any criticism. This became one of my new big hurdles. I thought I was being wonderful, so I would resist hearing more feedback from her.

I realize it's a trigger for me if she's got something she needs to say. Initially I'm not willing to hear it, even though I know I'm not supposed to be perfect. But when I'm stressed and I'm running from place to place, I'm less open to feedback. It's an ongoing issue for me.

I still need to be on the lookout for my anger. It's a lot different than it used to be. I can still cut someone off pretty quick or make it clear I'm not happy. I have to watch my impatience. I have to watch my thinking. Like if I'm doing the dishes and there are twenty-five spoons in the sink, I have to watch where I'll head with that. I need to take a deep breath. Or pick up the phone and call my sponsor, process stuff with him.

What has helped me to change was the realization that I was far from alone in what I had experienced and how I had behaved. But if I hadn't done this work, I really would have been alone. We were on the brink of divorce when I got into the program. I'm sure if I hadn't gone to the program we would have separated.

I have a lot of regrets about the years I spent being abusive. I think about what Kate had to live with—just the fear alone. From my childhood I know what that's like, living with fear. When we first got together, things were great. It could have stayed that way. It didn't have to turn into something so contentious. I think about the things we could have shared, could have done, the life we could have lived. There was so much loss of intimacy. Our lives together could have been a lot fuller and richer than just day-to-day trying to survive. Especially for her, while I was doing whatever the heck I wanted. It's a lot of lost years.

I'm sad about the impact my abuse had on my older son. The image of him crying in his high chair really sticks with me. I think he internalized some of those messages about what it means to be a man. Fortunately, he got involved with the program too. They have a children's group.

It sounds terrible to say this, but I don't know that I had a choice to not become abusive. From the example I got from my father, to the messages I got from the media, and the messages I got every day from how people are treated. You really get the message early—the message of how to be a man, how not to be a man, and who has the power. When new men come into the program, they can talk for ten seconds and I can tell their story. It's the same story.

What I wish I'd known was that the abuse I experienced as a child wasn't my fault. I didn't know that for a long time. I thought it was my fault. I've spent a lot of time processing my dad's abuse over the years. I ended up writing him a letter. I had him come to my group where I challenged him about the physical abuse. He was accountable for it. That was empowering for me. It felt very good. Now my dad is different too. He calls to check in about birthdays and holidays.

I remember one of the first things I did as a dad when I started to really change. My older boy wasn't five yet. He was really into fingernail polish. He was painting his fingernails purple. He thought it was cool. I remember telling him that was cool but, truthfully, I was uncomfortable with it. Then he got me fingernail polish for Father's Day. I remember thinking—"No way am I going to paint my nails."

A couple of days later, he wanted us to paint our nails together. So we did. He painted my nails green and his were pink. Then he went to bed and I thought—I'm taking this stuff right off. But then I thought about what we'd been talking about in group. I thought, maybe I shouldn't just talk the talk, maybe I should walk it. So I kept the polish on. The next morning when he woke up, he grabbed my hand to see if the polish was still there. It was. I ended up going to work for a couple of days with my nails painted green.

It was really interesting (and uncomfortable) to see people's reactions. It was really something. The guy I was working with was scared to death that people were going to think that I was gay, and that, by association, he was gay. I got to see where I felt comfortable and where I didn't. I felt comfortable at the grocery store, at school, with Kate's mom. I felt less comfortable with my own mom. I definitely felt uncomfortable at the Home Depot or on the loading dock at work. At moments it got a little scary. I was in line at the Home Depot checkout. The guy behind me looked like he could kick my butt. I remember keeping my hands in my pocket for as long as I could, until I had to pay.

It was the first thing I did that was public to expand the norm of masculinity. To step out of the box and not act like a traditional male. Men typically don't decorate themselves this way. I kept the polish on for two or three days. I didn't actually take the polish off—it wore off. It stood up to the rigors of carpet installation!

This whole experience also gave me a lot of appreciation for men who are gay. It takes a lot of courage to step out of that box. Sometimes people try to slap you back into the box. Even recently, at a PTA meeting, someone commented on me being the president—what's a *man* doing this for?

I feel a lot of relief that my boys didn't have the same dad that I did. I think this work has created a safe space for my sons to be who they are. I'm the example for them. I'm the one who hands off the legacy of manhood. Kids are better imitators than they are listeners. Hopefully, what they've learned is that it's okay to be who they are. My older son goes to a high school for performing arts. He's a percussionist and guitarist. He helps the little kids at the community sessions at the program. He's a pretty fantastic kid.

I'm proud of the relationship Kate and I have now. It's a partnership. I'm proud of my sons too. What both my sons know, that I didn't, is to respect their mom, to respect women. They also understand some of the privileges and power that are automatically given to them due to race and gender. I'm really proud of them.

If only I had known what you actually give up when you give up the power and control is virtually nothing—and what you get is immeasurable. You get to be free, to be who you are, to access parts of yourself that have been cut off. You get to have emotional relationships, to be vulnerable; you get great relationships with your kids. You get so much more than what you give up, which is such an illusion.

Ron Lenois

Ron was born in 1967 and lives with his wife and twin sons in Greenfield, Massachusetts. He works as a software engineer, designing health information exchange systems for medical practices. In his spare time, he coaches soccer, baseball, and hockey and is involved with the local Elks Lodge.

I grew up in a family of four—me, my younger brother, my mom and dad. It was a fairly decent family. When I was young, my mom was stricken with multiple sclerosis. My father worked at the university; Mom was a telephone operator before being disabled.

In my family growing up, my father was always the commander in chief. He was the man of the house. Mom was always expected to have the laundry clean, dinner on the table by five o'clock every day.

There was no physical abuse in my family but lots of verbal abuse. We had to make sure that Dad didn't get upset or else there'd be a lot of blowups. When Dad got angry, it was pure rage. You could see it in his face—all flushed, veins throbbing. He was also was very critical of all of us. He would put us down a lot: "You should know better," or "What are you—stupid?" Even in sports, if we had a great game, he'd remember the one play where we didn't do so well.

Everyone in the family stopped talking about how we were really feeling. We didn't want to upset Dad. Everyone would ignore the tension and hope it would blow over. It was never okay to disagree with him. Once during a dinner conversation, I took the opposing point of view in an argument about unions. He got so upset he left the dinner table. So I grew up learning not to say anything, to stuff things so he wouldn't get upset.

In school, I got picked on a lot. I was small in stature. In high school, it was worse; I was brutalized. I was a late bloomer when it came to pu-

berty. It was really stressful. I was active in sports but taking showers after games was really awful. I never dated in high school. The girls weren't interested in me. This really affected how I felt about myself.

My first relationship with a woman was when I was eighteen. From the beginning, I was always insecure, very jealous. In that first relationship, I started trying to control my partner. What I had grown up believing was that the man had the right to be the authority, to lay down the law. I had this idealized fantasy that if my partner truly loved and respected me, she would do whatever I wanted.

I was in six relationships before the age of thirty, and all six were abusive. I was always extremely possessive. With one particular girlfriend, I would go over to her workplace all the time. When she transferred to a different college and was living on a campus further away, I would constantly call her. I'd call her three times a night. I would use the excuse, "I love you, I miss you," but what I was really doing was checking up on her to make sure she was where she said she was. If I heard voices in the background, I'd give her the third degree. There were some nights when I would drive down there to see for myself what was going on.

Naturally, she'd be upset to see me so unexpectedly. "What are you doing here?" she'd ask. I would always respond by saying, "Why don't you want me here?" Then the whole thing would blow up. We had several fights like this. I'd always feel like she didn't love me. I didn't see at that time how I was crossing her boundaries.

During some of those fights I became physically abusive. I punched her in the back and hit her in the shoulder and arm. A couple of times I hurt her really badly—there were bruises. Once she was so sore, she had to stay in bed and skip class. Maybe she stayed home not just from the physical pain I had inflicted on her but also because of the shame of being in a relationship like this. I would use physical force as a scare tactic. I would intentionally break her stuff. One time, she was standing against the wall, and I was yelling in her face. She was saying no to me about something and I punched the wall right next to her face. I made the decision to hit the wall, to scare her. I was trying to scare her into a decision that I wanted.

I often minimized the abuse. I would say, "Look at how mad and upset you got me. If you hadn't done this, I wouldn't have done what I did."

I'll always remember the worst incident. We were having an argument. I attacked her—punching her in the arm and the ribs. After hitting her, I was still yelling at her. I don't even remember what about. I didn't get the answer I wanted, so I picked her up and body slammed her, really injuring her back. Afterwards I felt tremendous remorse and sorrow. I tried to make up for it by giving her flowers. It was the classic love stage in the cycle of violence.

I felt awful about myself. I knew this wasn't what wanted. I was a romantic. I didn't want to be like this. But feeling bad wasn't enough to get me to stop. I continued to be abusive. After a while, she broke up with me.

In my next relationship, my partner and I were inseparable. We were on vacation in Florida. One evening we decided to go out with our respective friends. We'd both been drinking. When we got back together, I started interrogating her. I was feeling jealous. The truth is that I had been unfaithful to her that night. But here I was questioning *her*, suspecting *her*. I wanted her to account for every hour. I went over her evening with a fine-toothed comb, wanting to know everything minute by minute. We got in a heated argument. She didn't want to answer me. I responded by becoming physically violent. I started punching her on her back and her arm. She was in the fetal position on the bed. I know she hated me for what I was doing. She was very frightened and overwhelmed.

Suddenly I realized what I was doing. I got off of her and walked away. I was totally confused about why I was doing this. I was upset with myself, ashamed about what I had done. I didn't want to go back and be seen by her or by her friends. She was totally afraid of me now.

We reconciled after this incident. I never hit her again, but I continued to control her, to interrogate her, to yell at her, be verbally abusive. I also knew that since I had already been violent with her, that just by raising my voice I could intimidate and control her. Eventually her friends stepped in and urged her to break up with me.

Two or three years later, I started dating one of her sorority sisters. My ex-partner warned my new girlfriend away from me. But my new partner didn't listen to her. She didn't believe I could be like this. Our relationship was still fairly new. But eventually my verbal abuse became part of that relationship too.

I've been arrested three times for domestic abuse, in three different relationships. The first was when I was nineteen. I had beaten my partner at least six or seven times. The last time I hit her, a friend of hers called the police. I was convicted of assault and battery. They gave me one year's probation.

The second time was when I was twenty-six. I was arrested for assault and battery. Again, I got probation.

Finally, when I was twenty-nine, I was arrested for felony stalking.

My girlfriend was at a conference in Boston. I went to her hotel and then followed her to the airport. When she saw that I had followed her, she filed a complaint with the Boston police. The police contacted me to say they were investigating what happened and that I should *not* contact her. So what did I do? I called her to ask her why she went to the police. That's when the police charged me with felony stalking. Then she took out a restraining order out on me.

I thought I could beat the charges. I would just go into court, clean cut, with my best suit on and beat the charges once again by getting probation. And that's what happened. I'd been abusive in all these relationships but nobody ever recommended that I go into a batterer program. With my first arrest, I got one year of probation. With my second arrest, I also got one year of probation. With the stalking, I got three years of probation.

Things finally came to a head in my next relationship. We'd just become lovers and one week later I had an incident. It seems that whenever I become sexual with a woman, that's when I start to become more abusive. It's like there's a lot more to lose; therefore, I become a lot more controlling. I try to keep the relationship just for us and keep everyone out. But what I want to save and keep, I end up destroying with my controlling behavior.

I started doing the same routine, checking up on her constantly. I went up to New Hampshire to look for her. When I found her, I pulled up in my car and started questioning her.

She called the police, and I was arrested for harassment. This was also a violation of my Massachusetts probation. Now my entire record came before the court. I was fighting to stay out of jail. As part of playing the system, I put myself into McLean Hospital for psychiatric treatment. I was feeling suicidal. I also got involved with a batterer program—my lawyer and I were trying to use it as a way to keep me out of jail.

I ended up being put on house arrest because of my probation violation. For nine months I wore an ankle bracelet. Throughout that time I attended the group at Men Overcoming Violence.

In the beginning of the program, I was just going through the motions. The program was just a way to get me out of the house and to look good in the court's eyes.

After attending the group about three months, something clicked. There was one particular session where we did an exercise called the "Act-Like-a-Man Box." This exercise really hit home. I started to realize a lot about myself. I started thinking about all the ways I'd been socialized to be a man. Between my father and high school, I was molded a certain way. I really believed that because I was the man, women should do what I want. At the same time, I was also being ridiculed for not measuring up. I realized two things: I was "given" these behaviors, these attitudes, these ideas, *and* all of these things could be changed. I didn't have to be an Archie Bunker–type of man.

So then I started trying to figure out how I could change. How *could* I be a different kind of man? I never thought it was okay to cry; to feel vulnerable, upset, have things bother you and show it. But it is okay to have these feelings. It doesn't mean you're a whiner, a pussy, less of a man.

Being in my group was really helpful. My counselor was really there for me. He was in my face when I needed it but backed off also. My other coleader was a recovered batterer himself. Seeing him there really showed me that change is possible.

Eventually, I did end up going to jail. I couldn't beat the charges. I was sentenced to a year in prison. I got out after eight months. As soon I got out I contacted Men Overcoming Violence again. This time, my motivation was different. This time it was for me.

There was so much I had to look at about myself. I was such an ass. It was hard to deal with the fact that I physically abused my girlfriends. I had been beaten up in high school, so I know what that feels like. For a while, when I really started taking an honest look at who I had been, my self-esteem really plummeted. The abuse I had done finally became very real. I had been in such denial about it for all those years. I had made so many excuses: "That wasn't really me. I didn't really do it. She made me do it. I'm not that type of person." But when I took a good hard honest look I had to admit to myself, "This is me! This is who I've become." The things I had done, I didn't want to do—ever again.

What I found at the bottom of all my abuse was my low self-esteem. It's what fed the jealousy. When I was physically abusive, I felt I had earned this. With women I felt it was my right to lash out, to dominate. I felt so justified.

I stayed in the MOVE program for about four years, minus the time I was in jail. I miss the guys from my group. I think about them a lot.

I have a lot of regrets about the women I've hurt. They probably all wish I was six feet under. I was pretty bad to them. I know I wouldn't want to be treated that way. If I saw them on the street I would want to apologize, tell them I hope that their lives are going well. I hope I didn't ruin their lives or scar them emotionally, keeping them from having a healthy relationship, being able to trust another man. But I've heard they don't want to have anything to do with me. It's really upsetting for me to feel that I may have caused lasting damage.

I didn't trust women, right from the start. Maybe it's because I saw my mom hide a lot of things from my dad. So I ended up never trusting the women I was with. But look at me! *I* was the one who broke the trust with them. *I* was the one who destroyed every relationship I was in. I think I always will be at risk for becoming abusive. I don't think you can ever say you're cured. You have to stay on top of yourself continually. I work hard to remain in touch with myself, to not allow myself to escalate, to not let my frustrations build. So I still take the "time outs" I learned in my group.

I've gotten to be the person I always wanted to be. I think I'm finally having my first healthy relationship. My wife and I have twin boys. I want my sons to grow up in a different environment than what I had. I now can pass on to the next generation what I've learned and hope that they grow up to be good and gentle men.

Darius Richardson

A native of Bermuda, Darius Richardson was born in 1967. He worked as the Program Manager of the Center Against Abuse, Bermuda's primary domestic violence organization, until September 2012 when his position was eliminated

PHOTO COURTESY OF PETER ACKER

due to budget cuts. The Center offers programs for both domestic violence vic-
tims and perpetrators and manages the only safe house/shelter on the island.
They also run anger management groups, support programs for pregnant teenag-
ers, and programs in the prison.

I grew up as the middle child in a family of three. My father was the as-
sistant pastor of the largest Christian Pentecostal church on the island.
He also worked as a contractor and was a musician. My mother was a

stay-at-home mom. She is mixed race; her father came to Bermuda from London. Growing up, there was a lot of physical abuse in my family, but we didn't think of it as abuse. We would just call it a "correction." To us it was normal—you'd just get beat if you misbehaved. It was a way of life. My mother comes from a large family—ten brothers and sisters—and every one of those aunts or uncles had the right to "correct" me. If I got into trouble at nursery school, my aunts, who worked there, would give me licks. Then I'd go to my Grannie's house in the afternoon and she would give me licks. When my mother picked me up, she would give me licks. Then my father, too, when he came home. Everyone felt they had the right to "correct" you.

Every child was disciplined this way. Your immediate parents would give it to you the worst, though. I'd usually be hit with open hands on my hands, legs, or behind, but sometimes I was hit with a belt. Of the three kids, I was considered the real terror. My mother used to call me a demon. I didn't see my brother getting licks—he was really passive, and he didn't get in trouble. A lot of what I did was just me being playful, but it was called troublesome.

Sometimes it went overboard. One time, when I was six or seven, my brother and I were on my parents' bed, sitting and talking. I was playing with a pen. I took off the top part and clicked it on my brother's head. My father went off—he beat me with a belt. He had the belt turned with the buckle swinging. The buckle struck me in my forehead above my eye. Blood was coming down. I remember him taking me in the bathroom to fix me up. He told me, "See what you made me do." If he did that now, he'd be incarcerated.

I spent more time with my father than my mother because my mother couldn't control me. My father was my hero. We looked alike. I tried to copy everything he did. Then when I was nine years old, tragedy struck our family. It was a national holiday in Bermuda, Remembrance Day, in honor of war veterans.

It was a beautiful, sunny day. We went on a picnic on the eastern side of the island. We kids were kicking a soccer ball around, and the ball ended up rolling down by the rocks near the water. I went to get it. But instead of picking it up, I kicked the ball, and it ended up in the water. I was afraid I was going to get in trouble. I didn't want to jump in and get my clothes wet. So I asked my dad to get the ball.

My dad took off his shirt and his shoes and jumped in the water. But just as he was jumping in, my mom became alarmed and called out to him, "Are you okay?" Something was wrong. As soon as he got into the water, he tried to swim back to the rocks. He surfaced twice, calling out for help. Then he went under the water and drowned.

Some other picnickers jumped in the water to rescue him and pulled him out. But no one knew CPR. Someone ran and called the ambulance. It seems like it took them forever to come. I was terrified. I just stood there watching the whole scene. Eventually, the ambulance came and took him to the hospital. We were taken to my aunt's house. An hour later, my grandmother came back crying, telling us "Your father has gone Home to be with the Lord."

A number of people said to me, "You know it's not your fault." But all I could think was, "Look what I have done."

Years later, I found out that he'd had a heart attack just as he jumped in the water. My mom sensed something was wrong—that's why she called out to him. But I didn't understand this at the time. All I knew was that I had kicked the ball into the water, my father went in to get it, and he had drowned.

A lot of times I wished I had died in his place so my family wouldn't have to suffer like this. I felt like I was in hell, and always thought to myself, "Look what I've done to my family." When I was eleven, I even started thinking about suicide. I thought, "I've already killed one person. Why not just kill myself?" I never attempted it . . . but I was in so much pain. I couldn't talk about any of it with anyone.

I started getting into fights with other kids. I would fight anybody, people bigger than me, it didn't matter. If they beat me, I'd come back right away and fight again until they gave up. I was in so much emotional pain that the physical pain from the fighting didn't mean anything to me.

At the same time, I started learning about sex. I had one cousin who was trying to teach me about girls. He would treat his sister so bad. . . . and I would join in. He would consistently call her stupid and ugly. She would cry to her mama and though she'd tell us to stop it, we would just laugh. This was just the beginning of the terrible ways I would treat girls and women.

I really liked one girl and wanted to fool around with her. But she held me off, saying she was going to wait until she was married. So I dumped her and went off with one of her friends—who by the first date I was having sex with. The first girl got all upset with me. She was hurt and yelling, but all I did was laugh at her.

That began my trend of being sneaky and hurting the women I was with. This went on for many years: I'd have a girlfriend, get all the sex I could, and then dump her for the next girl. I'd be all nice to girls at first, then when I was done with them, I would say, "I don't like you anymore." Naturally they would cry. To be completely honest, seeing them cry was powerful for me.

I met the mother of my first children, "Alvita," in church when I was fifteen. She was thirteen. It was my first serious relationship. When I was sixteen or seventeen, I broke up with her and went with other women. We got back together, but I continued to mess around with other girls. I graduated from high school, went to college, and became a police cadet. It was a way to get an education and eventually become a police officer.

All the while I would be two- and three-timing . . . sometimes having five girls at once. I didn't care which girl I was with. But then when one of them had another boyfriend, I cried like a baby. I was disturbed—I had never cried over a girl before. I decided I would never get this vulnerable again. I became angry instead. I decided, no woman's going to hurt me again.

I was twenty when Alvita got pregnant. We got married. Things were rough: the pressures of me being the only person working, as well as the pressures of life, would get to me. Alvita was going through post-partum depression, and I didn't understand that.

At the time I was a sergeant in the Bermuda Regiment (Army). That gave me a lot of power. I was still having other girlfriends. Alvita was feeling anxious and insecure. She would ask me why I was coming home so late, or who were these women making phone calls to the house. I became enraged, saying, "Why are you asking me this? I'm the man of the house. Why are you questioning me? You don't work! You have no right to ask me this!" I would be in her face, shouting at her. Or else I wouldn't say a word, acting cool and calm.

I really believed Alvita should be catering to me because, after all, I was bringing in the money. I would come home from work, and, if our daughter's diaper was dirty, I would explode. It might have just happened before I came home, but I didn't understand that. I just wanted what I wanted and I wanted it now. Once I punched the door and didn't stop until I had destroyed the door. I didn't even feel the pain in my fist until I punched a hole through it.

We were married for eight years. Alvita was always walking on eggshells, waiting for me to do something else. By now, I was working as a musician. That put me around a lot of women, and I continued to have affairs. I was emotionally abusive throughout the marriage and intimidating. When I got angry, I would curse, hoping Alvita would back down. If she didn't, I would get violent. Sometimes even during a regular conversation she would be terrified.

The physical abuse went on for five years. I had an incident at least once a month. I was never arrested, which is unbelievable. In what was the worst incident, I kicked her out of the house and locked the door with her screaming to get back in. Emotionally, that was really the worst for her. The kids witnessed the whole thing.

We finally broke up after eight years. My daughter was eight and my son six. I soon got involved with "Lesia" who would become my second wife. But I was still seeing other women. I just did whatever I felt like doing. One night, Lesia showed up at a club when I was with another woman. When she approached me about it, I grabbed her by the neck and threw her to the ground. This happened twice—it was my way of trying to get her to shut up.

We got married and my next child, a son, was born in 2001. I got back into the church, saying "I found Jesus now." I was training to be a corrections officer. I was trying to do better, but it didn't last. Because I was making more money, I thought I should be getting more respect. I started to do intimidating things again—turning the mattress over on Lesia, hitting the food out of her hands.

I was also abusive to my children. One time, I beat my older son really badly. He was at my house, playing with our younger son. I don't even remember what made me angry. I grabbed him by his school shirt, dragged him to the bedroom, and started slapping him upside the head. He got so upset that he started having an asthma attack. I could have killed him. Then I heard my Lesia's voice and that stopped me. I'll never forget the look in my son's eyes. It was like "Daddy, why are you doing this?"

I called Alvita to come get our son. She kept him out of school. If they had seen what he looked like, I would have been locked up. My ex-mother-in-law got on the phone and said, "I thought you were all done with this. You've got to get some help."

One night Lesia showed up outside a bar and confronted me about being with other women. I yelled at her. She said, "Okay, pack your bags and leave." So I went to the house and threw all my stuff in trash bags. Lesia changed her mind and asked me not to leave. But I knew that if I stayed in the house one moment longer, I might kill her.

I had been working as a corrections officer in one of the prisons. There were guys in there for murder, and I realized, "Wow, this could be me. I am going to end up behind bars." I knew I was a dangerous person.

I went to my Employee Assistance Program and had two sessions with the psychologist. He referred me to the domestic violence center. I met Mrs. Vickers there. I told her that I was afraid I was going to hurt someone. She told me about the men's program. When I found out there were some ex-prisoners in the group, I almost backed out. I was concerned about what would happen if they ended up back in jail. If they knew all my business, that wouldn't be good for me at my job. But then I remembered that I was close to getting sent to jail myself, so I decided to try the program.

On the first night of the group, I walked up what felt like a hundred steps to get to the meeting. Mrs. Vickers was the facilitator, and another man who had completed the program was helping her. There were ten guys in the room, including people I knew. Those men were shocked to see me. In their minds, I was supposed to be a Christian and a good citizen. I couldn't say a word that first night.

Eventually, after more meetings, I started talking about my physical abuse and intimidation. But the others in the group could tell I wasn't being totally truthful. The group challenged me a lot, especially whenever I blamed Lesia, complaining that she shouldn't have been shouting at me or asking so many questions.

Lesia and I were separated and were having a lot of arguments on the telephone. The group confronted me when I told them how I'd hang up on her or call her stupid. I would protest, "What do you mean I shouldn't call her stupid—she is stupid!" They'd say, "No matter what she does, you can't treat her like that anymore." I kept saying, "Well what about her and the way she's treating me?!" Mrs. Vickers was especially hard on me. She'd say, "You seem like a good person. . . . What happened to you?"

Learning that a woman was an equal was very difficult for me. Mrs. Vickers was constantly challenging me about my attitudes toward women. I treated women like they were my slaves. I felt entitled to do this because I was making the most money.

Our group was supposed to meet from six to seven thirty, but we would often stay until nine. We got into it deeper and deeper. I learned about "cool downs"—that if I'm feeling intense or about to explode, I need to take a break. I learned to watch my body language and to stop raising my voice. I was also asked to imagine how I would feel if someone treated me abusively.

I finally understood that I had a lot to be accountable for. I went to my first wife to apologize. But all the time I was talking to her about how I had mistreated her, I was still behaving the same way with my second wife. It was a complete double standard. I was being abusive to my second wife while I was trying to make amends to my first wife. My words didn't mean a thing.

Both Alvita and Lesia grew up in abusive homes. I had wanted to be the savior, but I ended up being just like their fathers, treating them in a way that made them relive their childhood. I feel sad about this.

I felt horrible about myself. "How could I have done this to the people that I love?" At the same time, finally admitting my abuse was a release, like a weight lifted off of me. The people in my group didn't judge me—which was amazing. The support I got was important.

I started thinking more about my father's death again and the impact that had on me. I also thought a lot about what I learned about being a man and a father. I was horrified that I ended up beating my kids the way my father beat me. My uncles were no better an example. One uncle told me, "Marry a woman who loves you more than you love her so that you can do what you want." I was shaped by all that. Though there were some positive influences—the church and the army—in the end, I still chose anger.

I had some intense conversations with my son, the one I had beaten. I apologized to him. I promised him I would never beat him again. I actually took him to a group session with me—he was sixteen at the time. He talked about my violence from his point of view. He told me that he was so hurt and angry that he felt like crying blood. Everyone in the group was looking at me and my reaction. I just sat there with tears in my eyes, listening to the damage I had done. I felt really, really bad— this is what I can do to someone that I love?

Over time, my son saw my new behavior—that was the most important part of my apology. I also explained to him in depth about what happened to me as a boy. He was happy that I was making changes and that I wasn't reacting like I used to.

Lesia and I got divorced. At the court settlement, I apologized to her. I told her that I knew the way I treated her was wrong. I would love to say more to her, even to this day, but she doesn't want to talk to me. I have to be okay with that.

I know I'm still at risk for being abusive. I have to mind my P's and Q's. I have to be fully aware of what might trigger me. If I'm tired, hungry, or dehydrated I have to take care of myself. If something triggers me, I have to make sure I don't respond negatively. There might be times when I might feel tempted to punch somebody, but then I say, "Wait a minute. If I do that I'll lose everything I've worked for."

After finishing my own program, I started volunteering at the Center. I was a volunteer for six years. In 2010, I was hired to facilitate groups. I also tell my story on a regular basis, do interviews on TV, radio, and the newspaper about being a former perpetrator of domestic violence. I speak in schools as well. I'm proud of myself for finally having a non-violent and faithful relationship. It means a lot to me to be sharing my story and doing this work with other men—but I know I have to continue to stay focused on my own life.

Robert Kurtz

Robert was born in 1951 and grew up in Northern and Southern California. He now lives in West Los Angeles, working as a sales rep for a manufacturer of high end residential doors and windows. He is a self-described "softball junkie" playing two or three games each weekend. At the time of our interview, he and his wife had been married for twenty-five years, with a nineteen-year-old son. He says this of his wife: "She's been through a lot with me."

I am the oldest of three boys. I was born in the San Francisco Bay area, spent my early years in Santa Cruz, and then moved to Torrance, near Los Angeles, where I finished growing up. I come from a politically liberal family. My dad went to law school when I was little and worked as an attorney. Mom was a housewife, busy with three boys to take care of. My brothers and I were wild. My dad didn't do much disciplining so everything was left to my mom.

There was always a lot of yelling in our family. I always thought it was okay to yell—that's just how I grew up. I remember my mom just snapping sometimes; she would go get a switch from the apricot tree or my dad's belt and just whale on us. That could really hurt—that switch. I never felt it was unjust, but it was pretty violent. I also remember beating up on my brothers.

I always felt that something was wrong with my family. On the outside we looked pretty normal. We had a nice house in the suburbs, my dad was a successful attorney, and we got whatever we wanted for Christmas. But my parents were estranged from each other. When I was eleven or twelve, my mother had an affair and wanted to leave my father and take us three boys with her. They made an agreement—she would stay and be in charge of raising us, but my parents would not be together.

Around that time I took up surfing and started going out on my own. I would stay with friends and didn't spend much time with my family. At thirteen, I started smoking pot, doing a little self-medicating. When I was fifteen, I started hanging out with people who were drinking and smoking. It was the midsixties so it was all around me. Then I started experimenting with other drugs. Eventually, by my late teens and early twenties, I became addicted to drugs—LSD, mescaline, barbiturates, and heroin.

The first time I became abusive was in my early twenties. My girlfriend at the time and I were both addicted to drugs. I had a couple of abusive episodes with her. One time I went around the house breaking things, on a total anger streak. I got into some trouble with the law connected to my drug use, and I ended up on probation.

Finally, when I was twenty-six or twenty-seven, I got off drugs. I was still drinking though. I had a couple of relationships where my anger was an issue, but I wasn't yet thinking I had a problem. I was more focused on my drug addiction and staying clean than on my anger and abuse.

My wife "Carrie" was originally my roommate's girlfriend. We started dating a couple years after I met her, when I was thirty-three. After we married, we seemed to have a really hard time in the first year. There was lots of arguing. Then I had my first physically violent episode with her. I was driving, and we got into a big argument. She leaned over and hit me in the jaw. I took her head and pushed it against the window. This is while we were driving on the freeway. It was upsetting to both of us. I apologized and promised I'd never do it again. Soon after, our son was born.

I got really involved in encounter groups in my late twenties. This is how I got off of drugs. At that time in California this type of therapy was very popular. The whole philosophy was "Never suppress your feelings." We were encouraged to confront people. I was never a passive person to begin with, so it worked for me. We had these weekend marathons where we were all encouraged to get all of our feelings out.

I always believed it was okay to yell when you were with your family. I was having incidents in my marriage every other week or so. I knew it wasn't okay to behave that way at work. But at home, I always felt like it was okay to yell and scream. When we would fight, I would call Carrie a "fucking bitch." A couple of times I pushed her when I was angry. One time Carrie threatened to leave with our son. I wouldn't let her take him, but she went away by herself for the night.

When Carrie came back we decided to go to marriage counseling. It helped a little but I would still blow up and lose it—yelling, screaming, and cussing. During one couple's session I got angry and started yelling at my wife *and* at the therapist. The therapist said, "I think you need anger management." That's how I got referred to the program for men with abuse issues.

When I first went to the group, I felt out of place. Half the people were court-ordered and had been really violent. I thought to myself, "These guys are much more out of control than I've ever been—I'm doing pretty good here. . . ." So in the beginning, I actually felt better off than the other guys when I compared myself to them.

There were a few people in the group I could relate to. They were there because they wanted to be there. There was one man who'd been in the group a couple years already. He was a doctor, highly educated — and a hothead like me.

At first I thought, I'm not like these guys. But, truth was, I was still yelling and cussing and screaming at my wife. I'd do it and then feel like shit afterwards. I would apologize because I acted like an idiot. But then I would do it again, the next time I got angry. The group taught me that I didn't have a right to do this, especially to the person closest to you. It's just not okay, even though I always thought it was.

I wasn't yelling or screaming like this anywhere else in my life. Eight years ago, I started working selling doors and windows in a showroom. You can't yell and scream and act like an idiot at work. I knew I should also practice the same at home.

Before the group, I always thought that anger was one of those emotions I should freely express. All those years of group therapy encouraged me to not to hold this stuff in. I believed that if I didn't get my anger out by yelling and screaming, it would just blow up and come out in even more extreme ways. Like that time when I busted up all the stuff in my house, I thought that was the result of me bottling up my feelings. But the group taught me that it's never okay to express anger this way.

One of the first things I learned in the group that really helped me was the "time out" — that really cooled me off. I learned that if I was starting to get mad, I needed to disconnect, go for a walk, to get out and cool off. I learned that anger feeds on itself — I would only get angrier and angrier as I was screaming. This strategy of using time outs really helped, especially combined with remembering that I didn't have the right to yell and scream at my wife and son.

I saw how my behavior was impacting my son as well as my wife. When I entered the program, he was fifteen or sixteen. I could see him doing some of the same things I had been doing when I was angry. I wanted to be a good father, and I knew in many ways I was. But when I got angry, I would yell and scream. This is what he started to do. When I thought about where he learned this behavior, all I had to say to myself was "Look in the mirror, buddy." I knew I was setting a bad example, and I felt really guilty about this. So this was a big reason for going deeper into the work—I wanted to have a better relationship with my wife, and I wanted to set a better example for my son.

When I got upset, I would take a time out and disengage. It usually takes me until the next day to be able to sit down with my wife to talk about what was going on. I learned that I needed to wait until the next day. If I tried too soon, I would still be angry.

I had to learn what situations got me going, what physical sensations I could notice that told me I was at risk for yelling, screaming, and becoming upset. I also had to change my beliefs. One of the things I believed for a long time was that I couldn't help getting upset—and that all of the sudden I would just "be there" in my full anger. But then I learned to watch out for my warning signs. Everyone in the group once believed we couldn't help acting the way we did, but of course we learned that we could. We learned that you can walk away. We do have a choice.

At first, my anger didn't feel like a choice. In the beginning I'd often say, "She made me do it. She pissed me off. There's nothing I can do." But then I learned there is *always* something I can do. I can decide not to go there. I can decide to walk away and come back to work things out when I have cooled down.

I've been in the program now for three and a half years. It's going better, but I'm still working on it. I'm not perfect. I still yell and scream, but I don't direct my anger at my wife and son. I had an incident about eight months ago—a fight with Carrie. We'd been arguing, and she went into the bedroom. But I had more things to say. I followed her into the bedroom, spoke my mind and went out, slamming the door. There was a button lock on the door, and it ended up getting locked when I slammed it. I was trying to get back in and couldn't, so I got mad. So I cracked the door frame trying to get back in. And I, like an idiot, had locked it myself!

I reported the incident to my group. I felt discouraged. I felt like I had been doing so well, and now I had gone back to square one. I had to realize this problem is still there inside of me. I've got to remain aware that I can still behave this way. It is two steps forward, one step back. I know I need to stay with my group, keep doing the process.

I do see improvements. I used to have an incident either every week or every other week. Now it's only once every couple of months, if that. My wife and I are in a good place now. We've worked hard to keep this relationship. We're both in it for the long haul. We've had our sad times and our hard times, but we're really a team. She's the one who said, "I can't take it anymore." When she said that, I knew I had to do something. She didn't threaten to leave, but she shared with me, in a really resigned way, that she wasn't sure we were going to make it. I feel that I was "wife mandated" rather than "court mandated" to the group.

This is my life's work. This is something I have to take care of in this lifetime. I ascribe to Eastern spiritual philosophies, and I believe that what you put out, you get back. Learning to deal with my anger is what my life is all about. It's always been a struggle. I've had thirty years of angry behavior—and the last three years of learning how to do things differently. I wish I had joined this group a lot earlier in my life.

Dave Weir

Dave Weir worked in construction for most of his life. At seven feet tall and 350 pounds, he could be very intimidating when he was angry. His abuse of his wife, Leta (her real name), was relentless. In one episode, he almost broke her neck. He was eventually arrested for this incident and spent several years in prison. After his release, he was diagnosed with throat cancer. He was able to be accountable to his wife and children and died one month after our interview. Leta talks about the healing between her and Dave in the last chapter of the book.

I grew up in Long Beach, California. My family moved out here from Massachusetts in 1959 and I've lived here ever since. There was my mom, dad, two brothers, and a sister. My mom stayed at home. My dad worked at the shipyards—something to do in the power plant. That's all I remember. My dad passed away a few years ago.

In my family growing up there was no violence. Instead, we would get the silent treatment from my dad. He never hit us. We got spanked once in a while but it wasn't abuse, you know. I mean we messed up. But he never just came up and started kicking our butt because he got

mad. When he got mad he'd go into his room or he'd just stop talking. And we knew to stay away. When my parents fought, the one that was mad would sleep on the couch.

We just never knew what Dad was going to do, I mean whether he was going to be in a good mood when he got home or was he going to be in a bad mood, and that was kind of stressful. I looked up to him, but I could never understand some of the stuff he would do and say. It just made no sense, and he wouldn't explain himself. I guess I picked up that habit.

I met my wife, Leta, when I was in ninth grade and never really knew nobody else, never had any other relationships. One and only, married for twenty-five years.

I became abusive early in the relationship with Leta. At the time, I didn't think it was abuse. But when I look at it now, I can see it was all about control. My problem was always about control. I wanted it all to be my way. If I didn't get my way, I'd get mad. I'd yell or pout. Or I wouldn't say anything. One time Leta wanted out of the car, and I didn't want her to get out. I broke the handles off the door so she couldn't get out. I knew I was wrong but I still did it.

We had our first kid when I was about twenty-one. I didn't know how to handle being a father. How am I going to raise kids, be married, and do all the stuff I'm supposed to do, when I can't even take care of myself? So it became overwhelming. And I just knew what worked for me was to lose my temper and be controlling, in order to get my way.

Over time, my name calling got out of hand, way out of hand. My verbal abuse was terrible. But, it worked. If I wanted my way, I yelled. I'd throw a temper tantrum. I'm 7' tall, 350 pounds. My wife was only 5' 2". So I got my way. I intimidated a lot of people, not just her. When I got mad there were no boundaries. I said what I wanted to say, and nobody stopped me. Not at home, not on the job site.

I started saying things that destroyed Leta's self-esteem, her self-confidence. If she didn't like something about herself, I'd zero in on that. If it was her weight or her hair, I knew I could hurt her that way. I'd just pop off and say stuff that wouldn't even be true. But if I was feeling bad, I would want her to feel bad also. So I would say things like "big butt," "fat ass." And when I saw her start to cry, I'd say to myself, "Okay now I know she's probably hurting as much as I am." Then I'd stop.

Leta's very smart. She went to school for geriatrics, straight A's. I knew she was smart and I would intentionally attack that, calling her stupid. Over time, my verbal abuse destroyed her. Having somebody that's supposed to love you say those things, it just wasn't right. I just wanted to hurt her. I was too big to hit her, so I decided I was going to verbally hit her. When I stop and think about it, it was all over stupid stuff. If I would have had any common sense, it would have never happened. I was too prideful to get help and accept responsibility. I blamed her for all my problems. No matter what, I'd point the finger at her.

We had two children, a girl and a boy. I spent a lot of time with my kids. I wasn't a deadbeat on that. I had them in all kinds of stuff. I didn't always run around like a madman. But when I was abusive, it was hell. They didn't like it. And they were scared, you know. They'd say, "Dads don't do that." I'd go in and try to apologize, but it just happened again and again and again. One day my son said, "I don't know why you say you're sorry, Dad, you're just going to do it again." He was just a tiny guy, and I said to myself, "Damn, I know he's right. The boy's got more sense than I've got." What he said really hurt . . . but not enough for me to get help. I knew I was doing wrong, but I continued being abusive anyway. In my own mind I could justify everything I was doing.

I'd say to myself, "If she wouldn't push my buttons, I wouldn't do it." Or, "If she'd leave me alone, I wouldn't have done it." After I'd been abusive, I'd want to just say I was sorry and have it all be better. Of course, it wasn't all better. Then I'd get mad because she'd stay closed to me. I would tell her, "Hey, I said I was sorry. What else do you want me to do?" But after a while saying you're sorry doesn't mean nothing.

Over time, my abuse became physical. I slapped Leta around. I can't remember these incidents well. But there were too many. A slap or a push or a shove. That's what landed me in trouble.

We had gone out to the desert in Nevada to visit her family. I didn't care for her mom and dad too much. So we got into an argument out there. I got in the car and I came home early. Leta and the kids stayed.

So here I am home early from a vacation that I didn't want to go on the first place. I already had made my mind up I wasn't going to be happy. No matter what they did, I was going to be unhappy.

When they came home, that's when I snapped. I'd been in a bad mood all day. Leta and I got in a fight. She grabbed her purse and was going to leave, and I said, "No I want to talk to you." I pushed her on the couch. I pushed her so hard she lost her balance and her head struck the arm of the couch. It was an antique couch with no pads. She screamed and couldn't get up. I had broken her neck.

I called for an ambulance. Leta was conscious. Before the paramedics came, I pressured her to lie. I said, "Tell the police you fell down the stairs and that's how you broke your neck." The ambulance came, along with the police, and Leta was taken to the hospital. She was an eighth of an inch away from dying because her neck had snapped. Miraculously, she made a full recovery.

I didn't get busted for the assault until thirteen months later. That's when Leta told her mom what really happened. Her mom called the DA. I got a call from a detective and a year or two later I was in prison. Leta had a restraining order; I couldn't write to the kids. I couldn't talk to them.

It was scary, being in prison. I was in there with the Bloods and the Crips and the Neo-Nazi's and the Skinheads. I remember thinking to myself, "These guys are murderers. I did what I did, but I didn't murder nobody. I hurt my wife, but these guys are rapists." I remember thinking, "Oh my God! I'm scared to death of these people. I'm sleeping all around them. They're in my room. They're right here!" But I never ended up having any problems in prison. I never got in a fight.

I knew I had to make some changes. I knew I had a problem. I didn't know how to handle my problems. I needed help. And so I just prayed a lot and thought that while they got me in here, maybe God's way will get me out of here. So I met some wonderful people that didn't judge me, didn't give up on me, and were willing to work with me. I took all the counseling classes I could. I got involved in all the good stuff I could and started to change myself, one step at a time. I worked on my control problem, one step at a time.

This is going to sound crazy, but going to prison was probably the best thing that's ever happened to me. I looked back on my life and started to understand myself more. I was always the bomb ready to blow. I was often frustrated. I felt I had a lot of responsibility, on the job, with my family. And I always felt the stress, the pressure of life, not knowing how to handle it. I was getting no rest, and I kept pushing and pushing. The more tired I got, the more of a monster I became.

I think also my size might have had something to do with my abuse, you know. . . . I was macho. I didn't hate women, but I could be intense when I was mad. I'm surprised I didn't hurt somebody a long time ago.

I said to myself that I've got to work on this before I die. I wanted my kids to know that I'm not a total jerk. I wanted to be a new man and, whatever it took, I decided I was going to do it. I got some books and really studied them. I worked my own program. When we had our groups, I talked about my violence. The other men would ask me how to make changes. I said, "Hey I don't know; I can tell you what works for me. I'm not a counselor, I'm not a shrink. I'm just somebody that's trying to change my behavior."

I got called in to the prison psychologist's office. I thought I was in trouble for something. He said, "I see the way you're running around this yard, and you're not afraid of anybody. People are always coming up to you. You guys are always praying, and there's been peace in the yard." I told him that I do pray a lot and ask God to help me. "God's doing some good stuff in my life," I told him, "and I have no idea what's going to happen tomorrow." I told him that men want to hear it from other men that lived it. They don't want to hear it from a counselor that's never lived it but only read about it.

So that's how I started my little groups in prison. I'm not a counselor, I'm just a listener. I could relate to a lot of them. I told them that I made good out of every bad experience there was. My mother would visit me and say she saw this new person in prison. She said, "You're not the same man. You're changing." And she wasn't afraid of me anymore.

After I got out of prison, I kept doing the work. I enrolled in a batterer intervention program. I also spoke to a lot of groups in the Los Angeles area, at detention centers and religious groups. I did it because I wanted to. I didn't have to, but I was tired of being a rotten person.

I learned it's all right not to be perfect. I thought I had to be perfect. It's all right to make mistakes. It's all right to cry, to say you're wrong, to listen to somebody. Other people have boundaries, I have boundaries. I don't allow anybody to yell at me, and I don't yell at nobody. If you can't treat me right, I don't listen to you, and visa-versa. I have no right to walk on you; I have no right to put you down. God did not give me that right, and I don't do it.

When I get angry now, I know how to control it. I walk away. It's just what I do. I haven't gotten enraged in seven or eight years. I still talk to guys about the ways I was abusive. Most guys I talk to are in the church. I tell them that God tells us to treat our wives like He treats us. I don't think God likes us going around beating on our wives. I say to them, "If you're doing this, you have to admit you have a problem and do something about it. If you're really serious about it, you have to get help—not just sit there and talk about it. You have to have a plan. You have to have a support group. And you have to make it work. You need to talk about the stuff that you did and why, so it won't happen again. You have to be honest with yourself. If you're stuck on stupid, get unstuck."

People sometimes come over to my house to talk about their problems with violence. I told one guy the other day, "You know, you have three kids and a wife who loves you and puts up with your crap. She doesn't deserve it. You have to learn to have more compassion, to be a better listener. You have to let go of your ego and your pride. It's not worth it to think you're right all the time. Give it up."

After I got out of prison, I started feeling sick. Eventually I was diagnosed with throat cancer. I think I got sick in prison. The water was bad there—it was contaminated. We weren't supposed to drink it, but they didn't bring in bottled water. I drank that bad water for two years. Other people in prison ended up with cancer, the same kind of cancer I have. I also was exposed to asbestos and lead on my job site. Between the prison and the job, I had it all. And there's no cure for that.

I never got back with my family. I had not talked to them for about five and a half years. One day I got a phone call from a pastor friend of mine saying that my kids wanted to meet with me. I felt numb. So I went to my pastor's house. My kids wanted to give me a chance. We spent a long time talking. That was good. There's a picture on my TV set from that day.

Thankfully, my son is not like me. He is not an angry person. He doesn't have a temper. He's an easy going guy . . . I know he got some counseling after I assaulted his mother, though to what extent I don't know. He hasn't talked to me about that.

Things have gotten better between me and Leta too. We were divorced about eight years ago. She lives in Nevada now. She likes to come down and visit me though. She knows me better than anybody, and she's not worried about my behavior anymore. She's very comfortable. We talk and we're all right. We have a lot of fun when she's down here and that makes me happy. That's the way I wanted it to be before I died. To put my family somewhat back together again.

When you throw love into the equation, miracles happen. Everybody wants to be loved. Everybody wants to be encouraged in a positive way. Some men never tell their wives they love them. They can't even say the word love. I was that way. I would say to my wife, "Love you, bye." It was just something to say. Did it come from the heart? No. It was just something I said when I walked out the door. But you really have to mean what you say. Life is too short to be a nut out of control.

So if I die today I'm happy. I've done what I wanted to do. I've been successful. I changed my controlling behavior and my temper and all other kinds of crap I had going on. I've beaten it. Not by myself, believe me. It's a lot of work, but I won. I didn't give up.

CHAPTER 2

The Road to Nonviolence

THE JOURNEY TO NONVIOLENCE is long and demanding and takes perseverance, humility, and support. If you are a man choosing to address your abuse problem, this chapter offers a sense of what lies ahead. If you're a woman whose partner has promised to change, this chapter can help you assess whether or not he is making progress.

Even when abusive men sincerely want to change, there are no guarantees. Many begin the journey to nonviolence but do not finish it. Some stop their physically violent and explosive behaviors but remain emotionally abusive or controlling. Even when they've succeeded in stopping all their destructive behaviors, this still may not lead to a healed marriage or to better relationships with one's children. For some families, too much damage has already been done.

This chapter describes the markers of change I have witnessed in the lives of men I have worked with and interviewed. I have learned just as much from men who haven't changed as from those who have. I have learned even more from my many conversations with women over the years, both those whose partners became nonviolent and those who did not. Additionally, my conversations with colleagues have helped shape the ideas in this chapter. I am sure there are men who have faced themselves and become nonviolent in ways that are different from what is described here. I hope they will come forward someday to tell their stories.

Although this chapter describes what the road to nonviolence looks like, it does not explain *why* some men make changes while so many others do not. Clearly there is much more to understand, including

- Does the severity of a man's level of violence affect his chances of becoming nonviolent?
- Do perpetrators of emotional and verbal abuse have more success than perpetrators of physical violence?
- Do men who admit violence right away have better outcomes?
- Do men with a more rigid view of masculinity have a more difficult time making changes?
- Do substance abuse, trauma, or mental health issues affect outcomes?
- Does the length of an intervention program or the curriculum it teaches matter?
- Do men with more community support do better?
- Does the age or education level of the perpetrator make a difference?

While we don't have conclusive answers yet to these questions, there is still much we can learn from the experiences of those who've taken the long journey to nonviolence.

The Long and Winding Road

Men who have changed have told me that the work of accountability and transformation is like peeling back the layers of an onion. They started by looking at the ways they used physical violence, verbal abuse, intimidation, and threats. But that was only the beginning. They needed to look at their subtler, but no less damaging, forms of emotional abuse and control. They also had to examine their faulty thinking which justified their behavior. Most came to realize that their abuse was not only about how they acted; it was also about what they *believed*—about themselves as men, about women, and about relationships. Ultimately, all of this needed to be transformed.

Each year approximately 150 men entered and exited our batterer intervention program. Each was given an opportunity to comprehensively address his violence and abuse and to turn his life around. Some of the men had initial interviews and never came back. Others started the program but dropped out along the way. Our groups always had this mixture: men who took the work seriously and those who were making only minimal efforts.

Among the men who were making sincere progress, there were always clear markers. Their initial resistance and defensiveness would change as they grew more comfortable and more honest. They participated actively in group discussions, disclosed more about their own behavior, and challenged others to do the same. They became more revealing in their descriptions of their abuse—progressing from vague stories minimizing their violence to more candid accounts. They let down their guard, opened up, and grappled honestly with the terrible things they had done. Over time we saw major shifts in their behavior, attitudes, and emotional states. Conversations with their partners confirmed these important shifts at home.

Most of our clients left after completing the basic forty-week program required by the state of Massachusetts. But there were some men who wanted to continue to address their abuse. We created a "follow-up" group for them. The group became a tight-knit community, a brotherhood of men supporting and challenging one another. When our first follow-up group was full, we started a second. Both groups continued to meet long-term, with men staying from two to seven years. It was these men who taught us the most about the long-term process of change.

One of the most important things we learned is that the journey to nonviolence is always a "two steps forward, one step back" process. The men in our follow-up group were deeply committed to change, yet also slid backwards into abusive behavior, sometimes once, sometimes several times. Even though they may have been abuse-free for weeks or even months, they could become abusive again if they relaxed their vigilance. Typically, the kind of incidents they had involved no physical violence; most often it was some form of emotional or verbal abuse. Nonetheless, any abusive episode was sobering—to them, to their partners, and to us.

The process of change is not about perfection. Many of the men in *Unclenching Our Fists* made mistakes as they were learning nonviolence. What distinguished them is that they *learned* from their mistakes and redoubled their efforts. They asked themselves: Why did I slide backwards? What can I do differently next time?

Though abusive men can learn valuable lessons from backsliding, this can be of little comfort to wives or partners. Most women feel angry, hurt, or discouraged by any new incident of abuse. For some, any new incident is traumatic and will be the last straw for the relationship. Clearly, a serious violent episode is a stark warning that the ideas and practices of nonviolence are not taking hold. If the abuse incident is less serious, though still troubling, some women may be willing to stay in the relationship while their partners continue their work. Everything depends on the severity of the incident, the man's actions afterwards, and just how much abuse the partner has already experienced. (For more discussion of partners' concerns and experiences, see the next chapter.)

A Map of Change

For a long time in the field of batterer intervention, there was very little information about the long-term process of change. Most batterer intervention programs don't have the opportunity to work with men for longer than twenty-six to fifty-two weeks. Abusive men rarely volunteer to stay in their programs longer than the required amount of time. But a few programs around the country have had more success encouraging men to keep going with their work. Because our program ran two long-term groups, we witnessed many of the phases and stages of men's journey out of violence.

There were very few guidelines available to us about the long-term process of change. Instead, we were learning as we went along. Eventually, by observing the work of our more successful clients, we were able to create a working "road map of change." We started with their initial disclosures of abuse and violence, how they became more engaged in the program, and how they moved from minimizing, denying, and blaming into greater accountability. We noted the emergence of genuine remorse, the use of tools that helped them maintain nonviolence, and the development of a larger understanding of their socialization as men. As we sorted through our observations, we identified three fundamental stages in men's journey to nonviolence: *beginning, deepening,* and *sustaining.* Each was marked by certain breakthroughs in personal insight and behavioral change as well common places where men get stuck.

This map was enormously useful in our work. It helped us assess where our clients stood in the process of change. It helped our group members see how far they had come and how far they had to go. It helped their partners assess change. We could see that the men who made substantive changes experienced most, if not all, of the steps outlined below:

BEGINNING STAGE
A man at this stage:

- Admits he has a problem with abusive and violent behavior
- Recognizes that his abuse is entirely his responsibility
- Understands that he always has choices about his behavior, no matter what the circumstances, and that he has no inherent right to be abusive
- Makes an immediate commitment to practice the de-escalation and self-awareness tools he learns in his group
- Takes a thorough inventory of the ways he has been abusive, including considering the effects of his behavior on his partner and children
- Examines all the ways he has blamed his partner or excused his abuse
- Doesn't interfere with his partner's efforts to seek support
- Participates consistently in his group according to his program's requirements, including reporting any abusive behavior, actively participating each session, bringing situations to reflect on, and completing any homework given

Common detours and dangers in this stage include:

- Any new violent, abusive, or intimidating incident with his partner or children
- Failing to take "time outs" or use other de-escalation practices at home
- Refusing to participate in group discussions or disrupting the group with passive-aggressive behavior
- Focusing on his partner and her "problems" rather than on his own behavior
- Frequently being absent from group and/or not meeting program requirements
- Engaging in woman-blaming conversations with other members, during breaks or before or after group
- Failing to report abusive incidents at home that have been disclosed by partners.

To successfully complete this stage, a man should recognize his warning signs and the situations where he's at risk for escalating. He should have reported to his group a number of times where he was able to *prevent* his abuse. If he has backslid into abusive behavior, he examined what went wrong and redoubled his efforts. Ideally, he will have had no abusive incidents for at least six months. In spite of whatever progress has been made, he knows that he still must stay vigilant and keep practicing his new skills. Because he is still at risk, especially for emotional or verbal abuse, he needs to stay in his program.

DEEPENING STAGE
In this critical stage in the process of change, an abusive man:

- Discovers a deeper, personal motivation for change, thinking more about the kind of man he wants to be rather than just responding to external sanctions
- Recognizes and commits to stopping all forms of emotional and verbal abuse

- Strengthens his practice of nonviolence, using the tools taught by his program, maintaining self-observation, and de-escalating whenever he's at risk for abuse
- Empathizes more with the pain and hurt he's caused his partner and family
- Allows himself to emotionally hit bottom and to feel pain and regret for his abusive behavior
- Examines his attitudes toward women and how his socialization as a man contributes to his abuse
- Scrutinizes his thinking errors and the beliefs that fueled his violence and abuse
- Continues to take responsibility for his abuse and to stay vigilant to prevent backsliding
- Brings any new incidents to his group, taking full responsibility and assessing what went wrong

Here are some common detours and dangers we've observed for men in this stage:

- Using the ideas of the program to displace a sense of accountability —for example, alleging his partner is just as abusive as he is
- Becoming resentful when his partner raises concerns or criticisms
- Feeling overconfident about his progress and relaxing his vigilance
- Expecting his partner to applaud him for his progress
- Failing to identify and take responsibility for emotional abuse and controlling behaviors
- Claiming he is abuse-free and no longer needs to attend his program, despite his partner's concerns and feedback.

Men in this stage should have gone one year without any incidents of physical abuse or threatening and intimidating behavior. If they do become abusive again, they are back in the first stage. There are three important objectives in this deepening stage: to address emotional or verbal abuse, to understand how they became abusive, and to empathize with their partners and children.

Men may spend several years in this phase of the work. To successfully complete this stage, they must have drastically reduced or stopped all incidents of verbal and emotional abuse. Additionally, they should have insight about the beliefs that have driven their behavior and the impact of their abuse on their families. Although they have made important changes they can feel good about, there is often still more work to be done. Most men may still have problems with some controlling behaviors: abusive tone of voice or body language, criticism, passive aggressive behavior, undermining their partners' parenting, or using economic control. All of these problems remain to be addressed in the final stage of the work.

SUSTAINING STAGE

In this final phase, an abusive man:

- Identifies subtler forms of control he uses, and commits to stopping these behaviors
- Stays vigilant about danger zones, watching for backsliding, and brings any incidents to group
- Is willing to listen nondefensively to his partner about her experiences of being abused
- Is accountable to others he hurt (if they are willing to be contacted by him)
- Communicates his feelings effectively
- Learns news skills for resolving relationship conflicts
- Adopts new ways to parent his children, including disciplining without violence
- Develops friendships with men who support his journey, reducing his isolation and lessening his dependency on his partner to meet his emotional needs
- Maintains his commitment to accountability by remaining in a group or having some other form of compassionate yet challenging support
- Practices self-care by making healthier lifestyle choices
- Recognizes that staying nonabusive is a lifelong process; that one is never "cured"

- Considers joining the movement to end violence against women and children by speaking out, challenging violence when he sees it, becoming a mentor to other men, and/or becoming a trained facilitator to assist other men

One of the biggest dangers of this stage is that some men will claim to have made profound changes when this simply is not true. Often they still have more abusive or controlling behaviors to work on, and they have failed to be accountable to those they've hurt. They may have appropriated the language of their programs to create the impression that they are abuse-free, but instead it is just another form of manipulation, often to achieve some personal benefit. They may do this to reconcile with their families, to get off of probation, or even to position themselves as a leader in men's work. Some have gotten a lot of media attention, ending up on talk shows or in newspapers and magazines as "reformed batterers." Yet when you dig beneath the surface, you often discover they continue to blame women, remain abusive or controlling in their current relationships, or fail to comply with visitation and child support agreements with their ex-partners.

Sadly, many people are taken in by this masquerade, especially partners who are hungry for change. For those who see through the facade, these poseurs only stir up more cynicism about the possibility of true change, doing an injustice to the men who've really worked diligently on themselves over many years.

By contrast, men who've gone the distance and made real changes are marked by their humility. They understand that if they relax their vigilance, they may be at risk of becoming abusive again. Men at this stage of the journey have had long stretches of living nonviolently that are confirmed by their partners. They have found more constructive ways to navigate triggering situations, express hurt and anger, and manage conflicts. This stage is marked by ongoing self-observation and the willingness to hear feedback from close family members without defensiveness.

The sustaining stage is lifelong. It is marked by not just the absence of abusive behavior but often an entirely a new way of life. Men who arrive here can feel proud of their accomplishments and the new kind of intimacy they can experience. Often they find it is freeing to let go of control and not be governed by their reactivity. They feel that they have not only addressed their abuse but changed who they are as men.

Unclenching Our Fists gives voice to a small group of formerly abusive men who have made it to this final stage of change. But how did they get there? In the rest of this chapter, I describe in more detail the most critical steps of their journeys.

Admitting They Have an Abuse Problem

Unless an abusive man admits he has a serious problem, he cannot change. He must realize that his abusive behavior is *his* problem, not his partner's, nor a problem in the relationship. It often takes many years for men to understand this, if they ever do at all.

For abusive men, taking responsibility for their behavior is half the battle. They spend years blaming their partners: *"She started it." "She knew that topic would upset me." "She has a drinking problem and gets crazy when she's drunk." "She has mental health issues." "She's the one who came after me." "She just knows how to push my buttons." "She shoved me first." "She flirted with that guy." "Her friends and Facebook page are more important than me."*

Most of the confrontations we had with men in our groups were about the ways they blamed their partners. We challenged them to change their focus—from their partners to themselves. "It doesn't matter what she does," we'd say. "You need to be in charge of *your* responses, *your* reactions. That's the only way you can make change."

Abusive men find additional excuses for their behavior: their jobs, money worries, their kids or in-laws. Some blame their behavior on their drinking. Some pretend the incident didn't happen at all or make light of what they've done.

Others acknowledge their behavior was wrong, but simply hope it won't occur again. The cyclical nature of abusive relationships can feed this unrealistic hope. Often after an abusive incident there is a "honeymoon stage." Some men make an extra effort to woo their partner back—by giving gifts or making apologies. But such gestures don't change anything. Things may get better for a little while, but eventually men with abuse problems will act abusively again. And, over time, the severity of their incidents will likely grow worse.

Given the multitude of ways abusive men minimize, avoid, or deny their problems, it is often only when they "hit the wall" and face serious consequences that they begin to finally face their problems. The men in *Unclenching Our Fists* provide some examples.

Ron, Chuck, and Dave were charged with domestic assault. Emiliano was required to attend a program if he wanted to stay in school. Robert's and Chuck's partners threatened to leave them. John's and Michael's wives started attending support groups for abused women and insisted their husbands go to a program. In Michael's case, his wife's counselor directly confronted him. James was required to go to a program by a professional review committee at his workplace. And Steve signed up for a program after nearly dying. Each man had some crisis in his life that sent an unequivocal message that his abusive behavior was wrong. For some, that consequence meant being put on probation and ordered to a batterer intervention program. For others, the turning point was losing their relationship, contact with their children, or their job.

I have never met a man who simply woke up one day and decided it was time to deal with his abusive behavior. Each man who succeeded in changing took action only after he experienced a tangible consequence for his abuse.

Consequences are critical, yet even when abusive men face them, many still don't admit they have a problem. Even though a judge put them on probation and ordered them to a program, they still find ways to excuse their behavior. I've heard group members allege trumped-up police reports and lying or vengeful partners. Some clung to the belief that their drinking or drug use explains their abusive behavior, even though we made it clear from the outset that one does not cause the other.

Every abusive man grapples with taking responsibility. True accountability evolves over time as each man progresses from being in denial to being more honest. In the end, men who have changed learned that instead of asking, "Why does my wife always do things that provoke me?" they ask instead, "Why do I feel I have the right to be abusive?"

Being Abusive Is a Decision—Not a Reaction

One of the most common myths abusive men hold is that they are somehow out of control when they act violently. This couldn't be further from the truth. Though they may be swept up in overwhelming emotions, they are still making decisions about their actions.

Men in our program would often describe their incidents in ways that suggested powerlessness. We'd hear them say: "I just went from zero to sixty in a split second." "All of a sudden, I just found myself in a total rage. I guess I just have a short fuse." "I had no choice—she came after me first. . . ."

During one group, a man new to our program described how in a "blind rage" he tore up his wife's blouse. When I asked if he tore up any of his own clothes, he looked at me like I was crazy. How had he come to spare his own clothing from his "blind" rage? I asked him. "I guess I was trying to get back at my wife," he admitted. "I wanted to punish her." So wasn't it true then, I asked him, that by targeting her clothes rather than his own, he was actually making conscious choices? He had to admit it was true. Another man talked about an incident when he punched his wife on both arms. "Why didn't you hit her in the face?" I asked. He acted astonished by the question. My coleader and I pressed him further. "Why didn't you just punch her in the eye? After all, you just told us how mad you were at her," we asked provocatively. He laughed uncomfortably and then went silent. In a quiet voice he admitted that he wouldn't want his kids or her co-workers to see her with a black eye. "So what you're telling us is that right in the middle of "uncontrollable" rage, you were making clear, conscious decisions about what parts of your wife's body to hit?" He nodded his head. "So then," we continued, "isn't it possible that you could have decided not to hit your wife at all?" Barely making eye contact, he nodded again.

When men finally understand they've been making *conscious* decisions to be abusive, then they learn they can decide to be nonviolent, even at a moment of great fury. Our program, like many others across the country, gives men tools they can use to de-escalate potentially abusive situations. The men I interviewed who were successful in becoming nonviolent told me these tools were essential.

It Takes a Village to Help a Man Change

Abusive men rarely succeed in becoming nonviolent on their own. For every man in *Unclenching Our Fists*, being part of a group where they were challenged was key to being able to change. Their groups helped break the isolation and secrecy that had long shrouded their behavior. Hearing other men talk about their abuse helped them to recognize — and acknowledge out loud — their own behaviors. Most importantly, they said they needed other men and their group leaders to hold their feet to the fire. Without these confrontations, they said, they never would have broken through their pattern of denial.

Interestingly, many of the men in *Unclenching Our Fists* talked about how their groups were a place they actually felt *cared* about. Instead of feeling stigmatized because of their unacceptable behavior, they could see it was a problem for many other men as well. They could see they weren't alone and that other decent men struggled with the same issues. They felt *supported* while they were being challenged.

I believe it is this balance between confrontation and caring that carries with it the greatest potential for transformation. Abusive men are more than the sum of their worst behaviors. They are best served in programs that simultaneously challenge them and believe in their inherent ability to do better. Such groups can become a brotherhood of the best kind: one where confrontation can be balanced by compassion, accountability coupled with support.

A Desire to Be a Better Man

Truth be told, many abusive men attend batterer intervention programs in a desperate state—anxious to save their marriages, to get off probation, to avoid jail, or get away from the scrutiny of social workers. But those reasons will never sustain men over the long journey to nonviolence. If they are attending batterer programs only to save their relationships, then they're likely to drop out if their partners leave them. If they're simply waiting to get off probation, then they'll probably stop the work as soon as their court requirement ends.

Eventually they will have to find a much deeper reason to do the work. The men profiled in this book all found it: *the desire to be a better man*. Although they looked forward to getting off probation, although they hoped to save their relationships, ultimately they were doing the work for themselves. In our group, when our clients would shift from saying "I *have* to come here" to "I *want* to come here," we knew they were on their way.

Ron reflected on the shift in his own motivation. "In the beginning I was just going through the motions. I was trying to stay out of jail. . . . I was using the program to look good in the court's eyes." Then one week, the group conversation on masculinity really opened his eyes. He started understanding how his socialization as a man had contributed to his abuse. Although he ended up in jail, he immediately returned to the program upon his release. "This time, my motivation was different," he said. "This time it was for me."

Empathizing with Partners

Of all the markers of change, one of the most important is cultivating empathy. Until abusive men can really understand what their partners have gone through, their journey to nonviolence is incomplete. Yet making the shift from blaming their partners to feeling empathy for them is quite challenging. Abusive men can often be very self-centered and prefer to think of themselves as the victims in the relationship.

Even when they acknowledge their behaviors, they'll often try to level the playing field, claiming their partners are just as culpable as them. Though they may acknowledge the way their children have been hurt, many remain unwilling to think about the pain they've inflicted on their partners.

My colleagues and I learned we had to push our clients hard to understand what it was like to be on the receiving end of their abuse. As a former advocate, I had spent years hearing women's stories—their fear, anxiety, resentment, the way they were constantly walking on egg-shells. Helping abusive men unequivocally understand their partners' experiences was one of my most important goals.

To begin this process, our program required group members to describe their worst incidents of violence from their *partner's* point of view. Most struggled with this exercise, finding it difficult to get outside of their own story. We asked men to repeat this exercise at least three times throughout their forty-week group. Over time, most revealed more details about their abusive behavior and were finally able to put themselves in their partners' shoes.

I'll never forget "Tony." The first time he told the story of his worst incident of violence, he claimed he had only cursed at his partner. Three months later, he revealed that he jammed a knife into the floor to intimidate her. In the third telling, he finally admitted he had held the knife against her throat. His voice barely rose above a whisper. At last it was clear that he understood her terror.

We'd also ask group members to spend time really thinking about the impact of domestic violence on women. One of our group exercises was creating an inventory of that damage. On large sheets of paper taped to the wall, we'd write the headings "Physical," "Emotional," "Social," "Economic," "Sexual," and "Spiritual." The men would brainstorm for each category; when they got stuck, group leaders offered more ideas. At the end of the exercise, their lists were comprehensive: fear, depression, low self-esteem, anxiety, hypervigilance, terror, distancing, hostility, substance abuse, isolation from friends and family, weight gain, compulsive eating, loss of income/career, physical injuries, reactive anger, failure at school. Once the exercise was complete, we'd sit in silence, contemplating the lists. The feeling of remorse in the room was palpable.

We also asked group members to consider the impact of their behavior on their children. A separate brainstorm accounted for the damage to children from witnessing violence. For many men in our program, this exercise was deeply sobering: they had themselves witnessed their mothers being abused. Now they were the ones inflicting the violence.

On occasion, advocates or survivors of violence would be guest speakers in our groups. Other times, we'd show a video of a survivor's account of abuse. Whenever abusive men had the opportunity to hear directly from survivors, it was powerful. As I recounted in the Introduction, Yoko Kato held the room spellbound when she told the story of her daughter's and grandson's murders. Listening to survivors' stories was another way some men began to empathize with their own family's experience.

Hitting Bottom Emotionally

> In the beginning, every group session left me
> emotionally drained. I felt like I'd been beaten up. It
> was just so hard to talk about these things, to confront
> these issues. I felt so much pain in acknowledging my
> behavior.
> —from an unpublished interview with "Tom."

Any abusive man truly waking up to the devastating impact of his behavior will struggle with how he feels about himself. This is not the temporary remorse that some feel during the cycle of violence. Rather, it is a self-esteem and identity crisis. I have seen men become depressed, anxious, overwhelmed, and even self-loathing as they finally face what they have done. I believe this experience is a necessary rite of passage for men becoming nonviolent. It demonstrates they have come out of denial, understand the damage they've inflicted, and recognize who they have become.

Some of the men in *Unclenching Our Fists* spoke about the pain of this self-confrontation. Ron shared, "It was so hard for me to look in the mirror, knowing what I had done to women. When I started taking an honest look at who I had been, my self-esteem really plummeted. For all those years, I had been in such denial about my abuse. But when I took a good, hard look I had to admit to myself, 'This is me. This is who I've become.'"

Men on the journey to nonviolence will often feel worse about themselves before they will feel better. This self-esteem crisis is not something to be rushed through or smoothed over. It's appropriate to feel pain when you've inflicted pain on others. We always made space in our groups for men to discuss the difficult feelings they were having as they became more aware of how abusive they'd been. Their angst was a necessary part of their journey. As painful as it was, their emotional crisis was actually good news: it was a sign of their deeper awakening.

When men hit bottom emotionally, it is important for them to remember that no matter how bad they might now be feeling, their partners have been suffering for a much longer time. Sometimes men look for solace or comfort from their partners while they are in emotional crisis, yet this can be inappropriate. It's simply unreasonable to ask the person you abused to support you as you finally feel regret for your behavior. Instead, men should look to their groups for that kind of support.

Every man's experience of this self-esteem crisis will be different, depending on how much damage he had caused and how deeply he allows himself to feel his own culpability. But after hitting bottom, the journey forward is always the same. By consistently practicing safe, respectful, and nonabusive behaviors and by being accountable to those they've hurt, for many men, over time the emotional crisis will ease. Still, there may always be some lingering feelings of regret and guilt for the damage that can never be undone.

Attitudes about Masculinity, Attitudes about Women

Although the men in *Unclenching Our Fists* come from different cultures and backgrounds, they have at least one thing in common: all were raised in a world with very rigid ideas about what it means to be a man. Learning how these ideas influenced their abusive behavior was an important part of their transformation.

As I discussed earlier, men both benefit from and are wounded by sexism. Just as women have had the opportunity to consider how their lives have been damaged by sexism and misogyny, men in our program also had a chance to explore how sexism affected their lives. We urged them to think about the ways they were taught to exploit or dominate women, as well the damage done to them by rigid definitions of masculinity. Our conversations would include the following ideas:

- Men are not naturally violent, but are often socialized to use higher levels of aggression when feeling attacked or afraid.
- Men are often discouraged from displaying parts of their personalities that would be seen as feminine—being nurturing, emotional, sensitive, artistic, noncompetitive—out of fear of being labeled effeminate or gay.
- Boys are programmed to keep their fears and more tender feelings to themselves.
- Men are socialized to take dominant and controlling roles in their families and workplaces.
- Men's friendships with each other are also shaped by conventional ideas about masculinity. Admitting feelings of fear, sadness, or depression to other men is seen as taboo.
- As a result of their training, men often feel emotionally isolated except with their female partner (on whom they become dependent).
- Men's view of women, either as sex objects or as subservient to them, impedes their ability to have meaningful, healthy, and equal relationships with women.

For the men in *Unclenching Our Fists*, exploring the impact of sexism was a major turning point. Chuck, for example, grew up believing that a wife is primarily there to serve her husband. He became enraged when M'Liss did not meet all of his needs and expectations. Darius, on the other hand, grew up viewing women merely as objects for sexual conquest, an attitude that gave rise to the abuse and disrespect he meted out on a regular basis.

Emiliano realized that his own views of women had been contaminated by sexism. "I had to face that I was sexually harassing girls," he said. "It was the norm at home, the norm on the street. In my world, women were seen as property, as sexual objects, and men would harass women constantly. Guys were always talking about their sexual conquests. There was no one saying it was wrong—everybody was in on it, including me. In order to feel like I was part of the gang, to feel I belonged, I had to participate. These were the only friendships I had, and I wanted to feel their respect."

The men in *Unclenching Our Fists* came to realize that very few men in their lives modeled healthy masculinity, if any. Not their fathers, grandfathers, or uncles, not their teachers or coaches. Additionally, there was a constant barrage of damaging messages about masculinity from the media and popular culture, from the sports world and the military.

"Between my father and high school," Ron reflected, "I was molded a certain way. I really believed that because I was the man, women should do what I want. At the same time, I was also being ridiculed for not measuring up. I realized I didn't have to be an Archie Bunker type of man."

The conversations in Ron's group about manhood and masculinity and their connection to violence and domination were eye opening for him. "I finally had a place to talk about the ways I'd been bullied growing up, how I never felt I measured up as a real man," he said. Feeling "less of a man," he realized, led him to possessive relationships with women. "I was always afraid they'd abandon me, so I felt I had to monitor and control them. I'd lash out when they didn't do what I wanted."

Robin said he learned to keep everything he was feeling bottled up, just like his father had. His father never cried or showed any tender feelings, though he was quick to verbally lash out. Robin realized, "It takes more of a man to admit mistakes and ask for help than just to pretend that everything's okay."

For John, the conversations about masculinity in his group were critical. "I got the message growing up that men are superior—we're supposed to make all the decisions and be the bread winners. Women had certain roles—raising the kids, taking care of the house, maybe working outside the house, but only as long as they were home in time to get dinner on the table," he recounted. "I got the message from my dad, and from the media, that men should be in control.

John said he also learned early on that "men don't rely on other men for emotional support." "It's okay if you want to talk about the score of the game, or go hunting or fishing. But if want to say, 'I'm really sad today,' another man is not who you'd turn to. Men don't talk about emotional issues with other men because if you do, you'd be thought of as gay." John's exploration of the impact of sexism on his life not only changed his relationship with his wife but his friendships as well. "I started to be able to have real relationships with other men— where we really know each other stories."

Men are often initially reluctant to come to terms with their sexism, usually because they fear they're just going to get blamed or attacked. But when conversations about sexism include the ways they too have been damaged, often there is more open-mindedness. When they see other men talking about these issues, speaking up about violence against women and exploring the impact of sexism in their lives, this can have a significant influence on men newly considering these ideas.

It's important that men not feel individually blamed for sexism, but see their behavior in the context of oppression and social conditioning. Nonetheless, every man *is* responsible for his own behavior and attitudes. Batterer intervention groups can potentially be a place where men can start to get new ideas about being a man in this world.

Examining "Thinking Errors" and Dysfunctional Beliefs

In Lundy Bancroft's groundbreaking book, *Why Does He Do That?*, he writes that the heart of abuse is always disordered and dysfunctional thinking. Unless abusive men change the way they think, they will not be able to sustain true change.

Our program was strongly influenced by the work of John Hubner, whose book *Last Chance in Texas: The Redemption of Criminal Youth* (2005, Random House) studied violent incarcerated youth. Hubner identified nine common thinking errors that precipitated criminal behavior among the young prison population with whom he worked:

- Deceiving
- Downplaying
- Avoiding
- Blaming
- Making Excuses
- Acting Helpless
- Overreacting
- Jumping to Conclusions
- Feeling Special

These thinking errors are often precursors to intimate partner violence as well. Every man in our program, no matter his background or behavior, always had thinking errors precede his abusive episode. Two types of thinking errors were most common. The first was based on beliefs of entitlement. ("It's my way or the highway." "How dare she defy me?" "I'm the one who gets to decide.") The other type of thinking error rose out of disempowerment or hopelessness rather than a need to dominate or be in control. ("No matter what I do, I'll always get screwed in the end." "I can't trust anyone." "Nobody gives a damn about my feelings.")

James saw how much his entitlement was at the heart of his abuse. He grew up expecting the world to wait on him. As the son of a doctor, now a physician himself, he thought that being arrogant and demanding was a normal way to behave. This thinking contaminated all of his relationships, both personal and professional.

Emiliano grew up in a neighborhood where violence was endemic, and he believed this was just the way life is. It was what people did to survive. In that context, he said, it was normal to slap a woman when a man felt angry.

Not only are abusive men more likely to make substantive changes if they understand the beliefs that drive their actions, but they also have the opportunity to replace them with healthier attitudes. Some say it's a relief to let go of their role as "head of the household"—to no longer feel they have to control everything. One man in particular talked about his pride in his wife's independence and accomplishments, mentioning that her salary was higher than his. He realized he never would have been able to appreciate her if he continued to believe he was less of a man because she was earning more than him.

Going Deeper

Abusive men can stop their physical violence fairly quickly, once they have decided they must no longer behave that way and keep using the de-escalation tools their programs give them. Stopping these violent and intimidating behaviors is the first marker of change. But overcoming controlling behaviors and emotional abuse takes much longer. The men in *Unclenching Our Fists* all made significant behavioral changes early on but realized they still had much more work to do.

James talked about his ongoing process of self-examination. "After I was able to get my more blatantly abusive behavior under control—the put-downs, constant sarcasm, and cutting remarks—I started to work on some of my subtle behaviors: the ways I wouldn't acknowledge people or even remember their names."

To be successful on the journey to nonviolence, men must stay open to ongoing feedback from the people who know them best. It can be a humbling process. They are often disheartened to realize they are still using emotional abuse or control. "One of the reasons I stayed in my group," James explained, "is that the work goes on. It's a lifetime's work. . . ."

Ironically, some men become *less* willing to admit their abuse the longer they've been working on themselves. They become more resistant to continued feedback, believing they've "paid their dues." They are reluctant to acknowledge they are still being even subtly abusive. "I thought I was doing such a great job that it made me less willing to hear any criticism," John said. "This became one of my new big hurdles."

Learning How to Communicate when Angry

Most people were raised with poor role models for expressing anger. Men who've been abusive are no exception. Although sometimes their abuse is more about control than anger, when abusive men *are* angry, they are often volatile. They need to learn entirely new ways of expressing frustration, hurt, or anger.

The men in our program usually had one of three dysfunctional communication styles when they were angry or upset. They either stuffed their feelings, escalated quickly, or became passive-aggressive. Sometimes they would do all three. Men who stuffed their feelings almost inevitably exploded later. Some men were just angry all the time, constantly operating at close to a boil, impatient, irritable, and quick to explode at even the slightest provocation. Others were more passive-aggressive—slamming doors, rolling their eyes, sighing, being sarcastic or mocking.

In order to change, each man needed to first identify his own "anger style." He had to make an ongoing commitment to interrupt himself when he was on the brink of this habitual behavior. Instead of reacting as he usually did, he needed to stop and think carefully about what he was feeling and find another way to communicate—without aggression, hostility, or intimidation. Our program taught men nonviolent communication skills as an alternative way to express difficult feelings and to navigate conflicts.

Men who are changing learn that all couples get into arguments and it's normal to feel angry, annoyed, disappointed, or hurt. But those feelings are never an excuse for abuse. It takes a long time—and a lot of practice—for new communication and conflict resolution skills to become second nature. The men we worked with were amazed to discover it really is possible to resolve conflicts peacefully. "It's such a relief," Tom told me, "that my wife and I can work things out without it all getting so ugly."

Repairing the Damage from the Past

Whenever it is possible for a man to be accountable for his past abuse and violence, he must try. Any hope of healing in relationships damaged by abuse requires accountability by the perpetrators. It is an essential part of the journey to nonviolence.

The men in *Unclenching Our Fists* all wrestled with tremendous remorse and guilt as they came to understand the destructive impact of their behavior. After so many years of denial and blame, they knew they needed to be accountable. They yearned to make amends, to take reparative action. They often felt a sense of urgency, hoping to heal their relationships and clear their consciences.

Many men on the journey to nonviolence try to talk to their partners (and sometimes their ex-partners) about the past. Over the years, I have heard about many of these conversations. Some were profound and reparative; other were disastrous. Sometimes men's efforts at accountability came too early in their own process of recovery. They became defensive when their partners shared their experiences, and the process quickly deteriorated. Other times, men dominated the conversation with their own realizations about their behavior, rather than making room for their partners' experiences. They were more focused on their own emotional pain than on the hurt their partners carried. Some women complained they were being pressured to grant forgiveness, feeling that the whole process still revolved around his needs rather than their own.

Without clear guidelines, even well-intentioned efforts at accountability can backfire. Men committed to nonviolence must keep two things in mind. *First, any efforts at accountability must always be governed by the needs of the women they abused.* Accountability is primarily for the benefit of those who've been hurt. Partners and ex-partners get to decide if they even want to have these conversations. *Second, even when men have the opportunity to be accountable for their abuse, they must understand it will not always lead to a healed relationship.*

FIVE STEPS OF ACCOUNTABILITY

An abusive man taking responsibility for his behavior should:

- admit that the abuse was his responsibility, without minimizing or making excuses
- acknowledge the damage he did
- listen to the abused person describe the impact his behavior had
- ask what reparations, if any, he can make
- affirm his ongoing commitment to nonviolence

For most men, their partners, ex-partners, and children are their top priorities for accountability. But for some, the process of accountability doesn't stop there. They discover that many people have been hurt by their abuse—especially their partners' family and friends. Often these people have spent years feeling helpless, worried, or angry about the abuse. Some men have realized they need to speak directly with their in-laws and their wives' closest friends to also address the damage in these relationships.

Additionally, many men realize that they've been abusive to others outside their families: co-workers, friends, even those in passing encounters, like bank tellers or store clerks. Though the degree of severity is never the same as in intimate relationships, some men have decided that as part of their commitment to nonviolence, they want to be accountable to these people as well.

Depending upon the relationship, the process of accountability can vary—from a one-time conversation to months and even years of dialogue. Sometimes, however, accountability is not always possible, especially with ex-partners.

TALKING TO EX-PARTNERS

Most of the men in *Unclenching Our Fists* had little opportunity to speak directly with the women from their past. Ron was haunted by this truth: he knew he had burned too many bridges. "I've heard they don't want to have anything to do with me," he told me tearfully. "I was pretty bad to them. They all probably wish I were six feet under. If I saw them, I'd want to apologize and tell them that I hope they're doing well. I hope I didn't ruin their lives. . . . It's really upsetting to me to feel that I may have caused lasting damage."

Steve did have the opportunity to be accountable to a former partner. Their relationship was devastated by his explosiveness, emotional abuse, and controlling behavior. In his batterer intervention program, Steve processed many of his worst episodes. After months of intensively working on himself, and with the support of his group, he contacted her, asking if she'd be willing to have a dialogue with him. She cautiously agreed.

Steve traveled to Minnesota in the dead of winter to meet with his ex-partner. They had a four-hour, face-to-face conversation in his motel room. Steve remembered how she sat close to the door in case she needed to leave quickly. He heard not only about what it was like for her to live with his abuse, but the way in which the damage still lingers. She described her ongoing vigilance, how she still flinches if anybody moves suddenly near her. She told Steve she was unsure if she could fully recover from the damage inflicted by him.

Steve stayed with it, kept listening, and kept taking responsibility for his past abuse. As the conversation continued, she eventually moved away from the door. "At the end, we ended up hugging," he recalled. "I think it was a gift for both of us. I'm not sure I deserved it—but she gave me a gift I deeply appreciate."

It was a different story with Steve's ex-wife. At their daughter's college graduation, Steve tried to have a conversation about the past but she didn't want any part of it. Nor did she respond to a letter in which he offered to listen to anything she might want to say to him. "I think she feels betrayed by me and my successes," Steve said. "She's had to struggle for a lot in her life as a single mom. Even though I provided money, she needed more than that from me."

It is a sad truth that some men who've become nonviolent are doing better in their lives than their former partners. Although many survivors go on to lead healthy, loving, and safe lives, some do not. Abuse may have undermined their economic status, self-esteem, and ability to trust others. Men on the journey to nonviolence must always remember they may have caused irreparable losses that no accountability process can repair.

Even when direct conversations with ex-partners are impossible, there are still ways for men to demonstrate accountability, especially if they share children. They can be responsible fathers, from abiding by all visitation and parenting agreements to staying current with child support.

ACCOUNTABILITY WITH PARTNERS

If a man is still in relationship with the woman he abused, it's not his words but his actions that matter the most. Being accountable is above all about staying nonviolent. Even the most sensitive of conversations about the past will be meaningless if the abuse continues.

Some men learn that even when they have remained nonviolent, their relationships cannot be repaired. I'll always remember "Shelley" and "Rick." Shelley was in my partners' support group; Rick had been in the men's program for nearly two years and had made enormous progress, going a long stretch without any incidents. I was thrilled by his progress and assumed this period of calm would be redemptive for Shelley.

It wasn't. Despite Rick's good work, too much damage had already been done. "After all these years, the house is finally peaceful," Shelley told us one night. "I no longer feel like I'm walking on eggshells. I appreciate all the work he's done. It's wonderful to see him handling situations so differently." Then she was quiet and looked down at her hands. When she looked up, her eyes flashed with anger and sadness. "But it's too late. I just don't love him anymore."

But for some couples, it's not too late. Once men have demonstrated to their partners they can sustain nonviolence, it's time to talk about the past.

PREPARING TO BE ACCOUNTABLE

Men need to understand no single conversation will heal the past. Accountability is a process that happens over time, often through many conversations. Ideally, men have already spent months in their programs reflecting on the emotional, social, physical, and financial damage they've caused in their relationships. In examining the full scope of their abusive behavior, they've hopefully experienced genuine empathy for those they've hurt. This is critical because *without empathy, any attempts to be accountable will fail.*

These accountability conversations are extremely important and need careful preparation. They should never be undertaken spontaneously, especially when they may be the first meaningful conversations men have had in which they do not minimize or deny what they've done.

In our groups, we helped men prepare for these conversations by having them write a "practice" letter, taking responsibility for the full scope of their abuse and expressing their feelings about the damage they caused. These letters were read aloud and group members would critique them. Eventually, the practice letters evolved into actual letters that were sent to their partners or that served as the basis of direct conversations.

"Tom" received a letter from his wife describing *her* experience of one of his incidents. He wrote a response, but before giving it to her, shared both letters with his group. "My letter was 180 degrees wrong," he told me. "The guys said I didn't acknowledge what I'd done, that I continued to blame her." After being challenged by his group, he understood what he was doing. "I finally got it," he said. "When you make an apology you don't excuse your behavior. You've got to say, 'This is what I did. I was wrong and there was no excuse for it.'"

Men often make two common mistakes when trying to be accountable. Some, like Tom, don't take full responsibility, suggesting their partners are partly to blame. Others have unrealistic expectations and are disappointed or angry when their partners aren't immediately forgiving. They want their partners to respond with tenderness or love; if they don't, they feel defeated and become defensive or even abusive. Rather than being patient and making room for their *partners'* feelings—one of the important objectives of accountability—they become flooded with their own reactivity. Such behavior can reinjure partners and sabotage accountability.

Conversations about the past are always emotionally charged, evoking anger or sadness in partners, shame and guilt in men. Men need to prepare for this, strategizing with their groups about how to handle their partners' feelings and their own. Because of their past volatility, these conversations are difficult, what our program called "red flag situations"—a real test of their ability to maintain their composure. Sometimes such conversations are more successful in the presence of a therapist or other trained professional, especially in the beginning.

Visiting the Craters: Conversations about the Past

"Being abusive is like being a bomber pilot" we'd tell men in our program, "and each incident you had was like dropping a bomb. Even though you've decided you no longer want to fly that plane, that doesn't mean there aren't still craters left over. For your partners, the memories of your abuse are the craters. To be truly accountable, you have to be willing to visit the craters with her."

Women bring up the past not to punish their partners, but because they want to be understood. When women feel truly heard about the abuse they endured, it can promote healing. Yet many abusive men go to great lengths to avoid listening to their partners' memories because they trigger too much guilt and shame. When their partners want to talk about the past, they often respond defensively:

> *How many times do I have to say I'm sorry?*
> *Why do you keep bringing these things up?*
> *When are you going to get over this?*
> *I'm sick of hearing about this.*
> *We were having a perfectly good time until you brought up the past!*

"It *is* painful to revisit the past," we'd empathize with the men in our groups. "Still, it's important. You have to remember that whatever

pain you're feeling pales in comparison to what your partner endured."
We'd remind them that every incident revisited is another opportunity
for them to take responsibility and express empathy. "You can't change
the past," we'd tell them, "but if you can listen with an open heart and
an open mind, something could shift in your relationship now."

We encouraged men to respond in constructive ways:

I really want to listen.
Tell me what you're remembering.
I see how much I hurt you.
I am so sorry for what I did. I can't make any excuses for it.
I understand why you are angry . . . wary . . . hurt . . .
    distant . . . having bad memories. . . .

Women may need to visit those craters for months—or even
years—after the abuse has stopped. Sometimes holidays, birthdays,
or vacations will bring up painful memories. Chuck stopped his violence in 1981, but three decades later, his wife still needs to talk to
him about the past. "She needs to share some of the pain she still has,"
Chuck says. "I did that to her and it's my responsibility to listen."

Making Room for Partners' Anger

Men on the road to nonviolence should not be surprised if their partners' emotions intensify as their own abuse lessens. Some of the men
we worked with reported that as they were improving, their partners
actually grew angrier. "I don't understand it," they'd say. "The more
I'm able to avoid having incidents, the angrier she seems to get. What's
going on?"

"This is actually good news," my coleader and I would tell them.
"It means your partner feels safe enough to express her feelings without fear of retaliation." A slow look of understanding would cross their
faces. They understood if their partner feels safe enough to express her
anger, it marks another important shift in the relationship dynamic.

Their partners' anger is a huge test for men on the road to nonviolence. Can they make room for these feelings? Can they listen? Will they become reactive or abusive? Can they avoid becoming defensive and respond constructively instead? Batterer programs can help men prepare by teaching listening and communication skills. In addition, men can practice responding to their partners' anger through role-plays during their group meetings.

Acknowledging Partners' Mistrust and Emotional Distance

Some partners don't express anger. Instead they are distant and withdrawn. Building emotional walls was their way of protecting themselves from the abuse—and the abuser. It can take a long time for those walls to come down.

Men trying to repair their relationships need to be patient. Though they may be anxious to reestablish intimacy, pressuring a partner to be more open and trusting when she's not ready is another form of abuse. Their partners are also healing and may not be ready to let down their guard with them.

Acknowledging the legitimacy of these feelings of mistrust and self-protection is helpful. "I know my abuse has caused you to pull away," a man might say. "I hope as I continue to work on myself, I'll be able to regain your trust. I know it's going to take a long time."

Many men who've been abusive feel insecure when their partners are withdrawn. They want to know they are still loved and still seen as good people. But as the relationship is just starting to heal, it's inappropriate to turn to the person they abused for comfort and reassurance. Especially in the early stages of repair, it's more appropriate to seek emotional support from the other men in their group.

Understanding Her Triggers

Even when a man has done significant work changing his behavior, his partner may still become anxious or vigilant. She might feel triggered by situations where he was abusive in the past—when she goes out with friends, stays late at work, or when they're paying their bills. Sometimes it's something more subtle—his tone of voice, a facial expression, or a physical gesture.

One survivor told me she was always on pins and needles in the morning before her children left for school. This was the time of day when her husband had always been abusive in the past. Even though he had changed, it took her several years before she stopped feeling tense and anxious in the morning. Men who are becoming nonviolent need to remember this vigilance was one way their partners tried to protect themselves. Vigilance doesn't just vanish simply because the abuse has stopped.

If a man notices his partner getting triggered, he needs to remain compassionate and understanding. Unfortunately, some men become triggered themselves. They might feel misunderstood or think the work they've done to change isn't being recognized or trusted. They might become angry. "I haven't had an incident for almost a year" a man might say. "Why do you still get tense right before we're visiting your family?"

Men on the road to nonviolence need to remember that their abuse is the reason their partners have these triggers. Instead of getting angry, those triggers can be an opportunity for them to demonstrate more empathy. "I notice you seem tense. Are you afraid I'm going to go off on you again?" Listening to what their partners have to say while providing reassurance that they're committed to maintaining nonviolence is another form of accountability.

Working It Out: The Slow Healing Process for Couples

Healing is as much about positive actions a formerly abusive man can take to nurture and support his partner as it is about stopping his damaging behaviors. It's about rebuilding trust, one day at a time, through reparative acts large and small. If sustained over time, his partner can begin to trust he's really changed.

For example, instead of sabotaging her friendships with jealousy and control, he can encourage them. Rather than feeling threatened by her career, he could become her ally when she's applying for a job or going back to school. Wherever an abusive man undermined his partner in the past gives him opportunities to support her in the present.

There are all kinds of conversations to help rebuild relationships, not just those about the past. Men can invite their partners to share their hopes and fears about the future, ask them about their dreams for themselves, their children, for the family, for growing older together. By actively supporting their partners' yearnings, many of which were thwarted because of their abuse, men can be proactive in repairing the relationship. This, too, is accountability.

It's a Partner-Centered Process

Accountability and repair must always be partner-centered. Whether reviewing the past, navigating triggers in the present, or forging a healed, intimate connection, men need to let their partners lead the way.

Sometimes healing emerges from the work a partner does on her own. A man needs to give his partner space—and time—for this. He needs to remember that her whole life doesn't revolve around him. Some of what she needs for her own healing will not involve him at all. He must respect his partner's individual identity—giving her space for her work, friendships, dreams, and aspirations.

Repairing a relationship damaged by abuse takes time. Here are five important principles men on the road to nonviolence should keep in mind:

- **Accountability and validation:** Continuing to take total responsibility for the abuse and listening to partners' feelings
- **Staying open to continued feedback:** Listening to what partners tell them about any behaviors that make them uncomfortable or that feel abusive

- **Affirming her support system:** Understanding their partners needs to have independent friendships and relationships with family members without interference, and to see a counselor if they choose, as well as have time alone
- **Making room for her to rebuild her life:** Giving their partners the chance to make up for losses they experienced from the abuse — getting a job, going back to school, taking up hobbies, and making independent decisions about their lives
- **Offering time and patience:** Recognizing that healing takes time, and not putting pressure on their partners

Continuing to Get Support from Other Men

For some of the men in this book, their violence intervention group became an indispensable source of ongoing support. "Without question, my group has been the most important part of my recovery," Tom said. "We're not afraid to confront each other, but we do it in a supportive manner. Even if every now and then it gets testy, we're allies — here to support one another." For many, the group helped them stay focused on their own nonviolence, to keep practicing the tools they've learned, and to be more accountable with their partners and families.

Some men are astonished by the deep connections they develop with the other men in their groups. They were used to competing with other men, never revealing vulnerability or personal struggle. For the first time in their lives, they could finally be real with other men, getting help for their struggles and offering support to others. Many said it was an experience of "brotherhood" unlike any they had before.

Other men find support in their larger community. Risking ridicule or rejection, several of the men in *Unclenching Our Fists* told their friends about their struggles with violence. "Everybody who I'm close to knows who I've been," Robin said. "And I *want* to talk about it. Hiding doesn't help."

Understandably, there are people who will not be supportive. Because of their past violence, men who are changing have to expect that some people will judge them. They cannot expect everyone to understand how much hard work they've done. This is part of the price for their past behavior.

Practicing Self-Care

Most men in violence intervention groups don't take good care of themselves, physically and emotionally. Their stress level is often over the top; this increases their risk of acting abusively. They often have no stress management skills, push themselves to physical extremes, don't get enough sleep, eat terribly, abuse drugs or alcohol, smoke cigarettes, indulge in reckless and dangerous behavior, ignore physical illness, and never go to the doctor. Men's issues with poor self-care exist in the context of traditional ideas of masculinity. Men have been socialized to tough it out; to drive their bodies harder, faster, longer; to ignore fatigue, injury, pain, and depression; and to keep pushing on. The idea of self-care seems either indulgent or "unmanly."

Our program educated our group members about the real consequences of poor self-care—men's higher rates of heart disease, high blood pressure, and suicide, and their shorter life spans. One of the program requirements, in addition to maintaining nonviolence, was for each man to do one good thing for himself each week. Many men resisted this idea but over time got better at taking care of themselves. Whether it was working out, going fishing, playing with their kids, resurrecting an old hobby, changing their diet, or quitting smoking or drinking, they started to treat themselves better as they were learning to treat others better. They came to understand that these lifestyle changes would not only lower their stress but were essential for staying nonviolent.

Remaining Abuse Free Is a Lifelong Process

Shortly after I traveled to Minnesota to meet with Robin, he had an abusive incident. After many months of nonviolence, he had a fight with his wife and kicked his car door while some of his children were watching. In an email, Robin shared with me that he was mortified by this relapse. "I stopped paying attention to my warning signs," he confessed. He knew he had to redouble his efforts and his vigilance. A few months later, he sent me another message. "I've been doing well. I'm continuing my interventions with myself. I've had no more violent incidents and the emotional stuff is way, way better."

Not a single man in *Unclenching Our Fists* sees himself as "cured." Some continue to meet in their groups. "I've been in my group for eight years" James said. "It's hard to be on the hot seat when it's your week to get called on the carpet for something. You have to really want to change and to listen to what's hard to hear. . . . Eventually, I'd like to get my Thursday nights back, but I'm not ready to leave the group yet."

Speaking Out against Violence and Becoming a Mentor for Other Men

Some of the men profiled in *Unclenching Our Fists* moved on from their own personal work to become involved in the larger effort to end violence against women. For them, public activism is the final milestone on the journey to nonviolence. Some have spoken publicly in their communities or at domestic violence rallies, conferences, and other public events, sharing their stories of accountability and transformation. Some have recounted their stories in newspapers or on television, like Chuck and his wife M'Liss , who appeared on *The Phil Donahue Show* and *Oprah*. Another man in the book, Steve, was also a guest on *Oprah*.

Others began working with men who are abusive. A few have become group leaders or mentors in abuse intervention programs. Some, like Emiliano, have taken major leadership roles, working across Texas educating young people about healthy relationships in an effort to prevent future acts of sexual and domestic violence.

While some men work publicly, others are role models in their personal lives and communities. By talking openly with friends, neighbors, and coworkers, men who have changed often inspire others to consider their own abuse and violence. Sometimes former perpetrators will intentionally seek out men they know need help with this issue. These friend-to-friend conversations are very important—many men entered our program only because a friend challenged them to face their problems.

Men who were once abusive have the potential to become effective leaders in the work of challenging violence against women. Former perpetrators have a unique voice and an authentic authority because they've "walked their talk." They show other men what is possible for their own lives.

All of the men in *Unclenching Our Fists* understand they can never erase the hurt they once inflicted. But, they told me, they hope that their stories will inspire other men to address their violence and keep some women and children a little safer. "If only one good thing could come out of my struggle with abuse," Robin said, "it would be that my story helps someone else."

CHAPTER THREE

When the Man You Love Is Abusive

I F YOUR PARTNER HAS been abusive, you're no doubt wondering, "Can he stop his abuse like the men in this book have?" Although the stories in *Unclenching Our Fists* show change *is* possible, it's important to balance the hopes you have for your relationship with caution. The previous chapter detailed the process men go through to become nonviolent and to be accountable to those they have hurt. This chapter, written for partners, synthesizes the essential elements women hoping for change should consider.

Many Abusive Men Do Not Become Nonviolent

Only a small number of men with abuse issues put in the time and effort to make substantive changes. Most abusive men do not address their issues. They do not enroll in batterer intervention programs or seek the help of therapists. Even when they do, many don't make the changes their partners are longing for. In my home state of Massachusetts, *half* of all men who enroll in programs drop out.

Among the men who *do* complete programs, some may remain emotionally abusive or become physically violent after they stop attending. Successful program completion is never a guarantee that there will be no future violence.

I realize this is not encouraging news. The process of dismantling abusive behavior is fraught with setbacks. Yet, like dandelions push-ing up through asphalt, there are success stories. There are men who have chosen to change their lives and stop their violence. In the end, it comes down to choice. The man you're with must make that choice — to stop his abuse, get help, and keep working on himself.

Attending a Domestic Violence Intervention Program Is Essential

Men with abuse problems don't change in isolation. They need a place where, as James said, their "feet will be held to the fire." They need people who will challenge their behaviors and attitudes and show them ways they can handle things better.

As discussed earlier, abusive men have the greatest chance of suc-cess when they work with others who have the same issues. A group breaks down the isolation, stigma, and secrecy surrounding abusive be-havior. Men are exposed to others who are farther along in the work and who have accepted responsibility for their behavior. Hearing other men's stories, learning about the various types of domestic abuse, being challenged by group leaders, and practicing tools for nonviolence are all critical to any process of change.

Sometimes only external crises or sanctions — an arrest, a restrain-ing order, child protective services — will get men into a program. Some men do enter programs voluntarily, often because they have separated from their partners or because their partners insist that they get help.

A batterer intervention program is far more preferable than an an-ger management program. Batterer programs are longer and more comprehensive, and understand that abuse is not just about anger, but also about coercion and control. (See "Batterer Intervention: The Big Picture" in Chapter 1 for more discussion of the difference between the two types of programs.)

It is not your responsibility to get your partner enrolled in a group. The responsibility for enrolling is his and his alone. However, many times women are the ones who find out about their local programs and pressure their partners to get help. If you feel safe enough, you can write down the phone number, but he has to make the call.

Whether your partner ends up in a group or with an individual therapist experienced with intimate partner abuse, make sure you have a chance to be interviewed confidentially about your experience. Since abusive men tend to minimize and deny their behavior, it is essential your experiences are included in any assessment. Many batterer intervention programs have partner specialists who will contact you to learn about your experience as well as to answer your questions. This contact is critical and is another reason why anger management programs are insufficient—they rarely reach out to partners to gain their perspective.

If He Doesn't "Own" His Problems, He Can't Change Them

Once he has sought help, his next tasks are to accept full responsibility for his abuse and commit to nonviolence. This means he has to stop blaming you and others for the way he behaves.

Sometimes, in the aftermath of an abusive episode, some men will be flooded with guilt and remorse about their behavior. It's a crack in their wall of denial, letting in the light of the truth. But as time passes, they often slip back into minimizing what they've done or blaming you. Eventually they become abusive again. This is the cycle of violence. In the end, nothing changes.

Abusive men cannot afford slip back into complacency. If they feel bad about their behavior, they must use that remorse to fuel them to take action. They must learn to take full responsibility for their abuse and practice strategies that will help them remain nonviolent, one day at a time.

The best action partners can take is to insist that men stick with their programs. Don't rush to make things better or sweep the abuse under the rug. Understand that the process of change takes time. It's not a sprint—it's a marathon.

Substance Abuse Is a Separate Issue

If your partner also has a substance abuse problem, getting sober is essential, but sobriety alone will not stop the abuse. Contrary to popular belief, alcohol or drugs do not cause a man to be abusive. However, substance abuse can exacerbate the violence and put you at greater risk of injury. Unfortunately, many men who become sober remain abusive. A man who is violent and also abuses substances has two problems to address.

Couples' Counseling Is Inappropriate

Couples' counseling is not an appropriate intervention for men beginning to address their abusive behavior. Your partner may lobby hard for such counseling (even as a substitute for a group), but at this early stage, it is rarely successful. Abuse is a problem in the abuser, not a problem in the relationship. Couples' counseling allows him to criticize your behavior rather than focusing on his own. Many therapists inexperienced in the dynamics of domestic abuse may reinforce the misguided notion that you share some responsibility for *his* violence.

Additionally, couples' counseling can be risky. A man who hasn't yet taken responsibility for his abuse might retaliate against his partner for what she says in the session. Some women have reported being abused immediately after leaving the therapist's office.

Couple's counseling can eventually be helpful, but your partner should be abuse free for some time before you consider it. Make sure any therapist you work with has a thorough understanding of the dynamics of intimate partner abuse.

Keep Your Guard Up; Change Takes Time

Once your partner has entered a program, it is natural to breathe a sigh of relief. Still, remember this is only a first step. Whether his efforts will result in substantive change remains to be seen. Your partner was not born abusive. Through a complex series of influences and experiences, he learned to become abusive. It took years for those behaviors to become embedded in him; unlearning them will also take time.

His first priority should be recognizing when he is at risk of being abusive or violent and stopping himself from acting out those behaviors. After he's learned to prevent his abuse, there's still more work to be done. Changing behavior is only the beginning. He must also address the thinking and belief systems that he has long used to justify his abuse and control.

Once your partner has gone a stretch of time without an incident, he may feel tempted to assert he is now "recovered." But a few months of "good behavior," after years of abuse, is too soon to proclaim victory.

Men committed to change should feel good about their successes. They should feel proud about the times they have prevented incidents. But this pride must be tempered by recognizing there is more work to be done. Even if they've stopped many types of abusive behaviors, there may still be more subtle forms of controlling behavior and emotional abuse for them to confront and change.

Two Steps Forward, One Step Back

Even men who have committed to change can still slide backwards into old behaviors. Naturally, this is upsetting to any partner impatient for the abuse to end.

You are not expected to tolerate serious physical violence as part of his "recovery." If he is abusive again, the way you respond will depend on the severity of his incident. A new violent incident is often the "last straw" for many women. But a less serious incident may not have the same devastating impact. For many partners, there's a big difference between him slamming a door in anger versus being pushed or slapped. Women have told me that if their partners had been nonviolent for a long time, they felt they could tolerate a minor episode of backsliding because so much progress had been made. However, they still needed their partners to take full responsibility for their behavior and to redouble their efforts.

If a man has an abusive incident while enrolled in his program, it's essential he disclose it in his group. He needs to analyze what happened and understand what he could have done differently. Any new abusive incident is clearly a setback, yet with the help of his group, he can learn something essential and be better able to prevent future incidents.

Some men committed to change are able to move forward with little backsliding. Others veer back and forth between healthy and abusive behavior. Some sustain nonviolence for a long time only to completely regress during a stressful period in their lives.

For some women, *any* new abusive incident is painful and damaging. They may be so fed up or exhausted by what they've already gone through, they may not be willing to weather another storm. Others may choose to remain in the relationship while their partners are on the bumpy road to recovery.

The Markers of Change:
Your Own Experience Matters Most

In the end, it is your experience that determines whether your partner has changed. No matter what the counselors in his program think of his progress, what's most important is what you feel and know. Take a look at the following checklists, culled from the experiences of survivors and advocates. (Many thanks to the Emerge Program of Cambridge, MA, for first articulating many of the ideas listed here.)

SIGNS HE *Is* CHANGING
- He has stopped being violent or threatening to you or others.
- He acknowledges his abusive behavior is wrong.
- He understands he does not have the right to control and dominate you.
- You don't feel like you're "walking on eggshells" when you are with him.
- He respects your wishes about sex and physical contact.

- You can express anger and frustration toward him without feeling intimidated and without him escalating into abuse.
- He does not make you feel responsible for his abuse.
- He consistently practices the skills and tools he's learned in his group.
- He respects your opinion, even if he doesn't always agree with it.
- He respects your right to say "no."
- You can negotiate with him without being humiliated and belittled.
- When you're concerned that his anger is escalating, he listens to you and takes action to prevent becoming abusive.
- You don't have to ask his permission to go out, go back to school, or get a job.
- He listens to you and respects what you have to say.
- He communicates honestly, without trying to manipulate you.
- He recognizes he is not "cured" and that changing his behavior, attitudes, and beliefs is a lifelong process.
- He is willing to listen to you talk about the past without becoming defensive.
- He no longer does _____ (*fill in any abusive behavior of his not included in the list*).

SIGNS HE IS *Not* CHANGING

- He tries to entice you with romantic gifts, dinners, and flowers but does not enroll in a treatment program.
- He attends his group sporadically or drops out before completion.
- He tries to invoke sympathy from you or others, or presents himself as the victim.
- He expects your immediate trust, love, and physical intimacy simply because he's in a program.
- He expects you to forgive him immediately for what he's done and becomes angry when you don't.
- He expects you to applaud his progress and praise him when he's not abusive.
- He tells you that he's not nearly as bad as the other guys in his group.

- He uses curriculum from his program to argue that you also have an abuse problem.
- He tells you that when he's completed the program, he'll be cured.
- He puts pressure on you to take him back, to drop a restraining order or criminal charges, to suspend divorce proceedings, or to attend couples' counseling or therapy for yourself.
- He uses veiled threats—to take the kids away, to quit attending his program, to cut off financial support.
- He tells you, "We need to stay together" for him to work on his problems.

Healing Yourself No Matter What He Does

Whether or not the man you love changes, you deserve to live a healthy life. It is important you focus on your own wellbeing, no matter what he does. One of the common dynamics of an abusive relationship (and any unhealthy relationship) is that much of your energy and attention is consumed by his problems. You've long been enduring his abuse with its attendant uncertainty, fear, hurt, and anxiety. Perhaps you believed it was your responsibility to get him to face his problems. If he's enrolled in a program, his group leaders are now responsible to help him face his behavior. You can finally pay more attention to yourself.

Abuse deeply damages a woman's life: emotionally, physically, economically, socially, and spiritually. Healing from abuse is a topic that deserves far more discussion than space in this chapter allows. There are excellent resources for survivors, including domestic violence programs, books, helplines, online chat rooms, and blogs. Please see the bibliography for suggestions and resources about how you can get support.

Please remember:

- The abuse was *never* your fault, no matter what he said.
- It's important to take stock of all the ways his abuse impacted your life.
- Don't forget your strengths—you wouldn't have survived without them.

- Stay connected to those who care about you. Make sure they understand the complexities of intimate partner abuse and will not judge you.
- Begin to reclaim what you had to give up.
- Decide you will live without abuse or violence, no matter what he does.

You Deserve a Supportive Community

It is critical to have knowledgeable and nonjudgmental support if you've been in an abusive relationship. Sometimes close friends and family members can provide that support, but other times a support group with other women who are also in abusive relationships can be profoundly helpful. Over my many years in this work, I have seen that women are more easily able to recover their strength in the company of other women. The support, insight, and caring from those who have also lived with abuse is priceless.

Still, some women are reluctant to join a support group. Some feel uncomfortable sharing such a personal, painful experience with people they don't know. Others assume that support groups for battered women are only for victims of physical violence. Others stay away from groups because they don't identify with the stereotypical image of a "battered woman."

Though we now know that all kinds of women from all kinds of backgrounds can find themselves in abusive relationships, stereotypes about battered women—as impoverished, undereducated, covered with bruises—still exist. The women I've worked with over the years rarely fit this or any stereotype. They came from all segments of society and cut across class, race, and ethnicity. They discovered that abuse can and does happen to anyone. They understood that abuse is far more than just physical. They needn't have broken bones and black eyes to have had their lives shattered and their self-esteem undermined. Support groups help women identify the emotional and psychological abuse they experienced and to understand fully just how damaging and crazy-making it was. In these groups, women's experiences are believed and validated.

For some women, joining a group is not possible: there are none nearby, there are family or logistical conflicts, or they're just not comfortable being in a group environment. Even women who do join a group may need additional support. For all of these reasons, seeing an individual counselor with experience in intimate partner abuse may be helpful. Some women report that one-on-one counseling was key to their recovery.

Unfortunately, some well-intentioned therapists have narrow ideas of what the best outcome is for a woman in an abusive relationship. Some faith-based counselors reject the option of separation or divorce. Some battered women's counselors who don't think abusive men can ever change may advocate separation as the only way a woman can be safe. It's important to ask a prospective therapist about her experience working with women who've made both the choice to stay and the choice to leave.

In addition to emotional support, abuse survivors often need other forms of help—from legal and economic assistance to housing and services for their children. Programs for abused women can provide all of this: a twenty-four-hour crisis hotline, legal advocacy, pro bono lawyers or attorney referrals, support for children, personal and financial advocacy, safety planning, and, if necessary, safe shelter. These services are usually free. A national domestic abuse hotline, listed in the appendix, can help you locate a program in your area. Also listed are helpful websites and books about healing from abuse.

So much gets stolen by abuse. You might feel it's too hard to remember the woman you once were. But that woman is still alive in you, and you can reclaim her. You can make your life whole again, one step at a time.

Commit to an Abuse-Free Life

Across the country, many cities and towns have declared themselves "Domestic Violence–Free Zones." Local police receive training to more effectively respond to domestic violence incidents. Schools and faith communities are involved in prevention and education efforts.

Services exist to support victims and hold perpetrators accountable. In a coordinated system of response, community task forces bring together the courts, police, battered women's shelters, and batterer intervention programs. A "Domestic Violence–Free Zone" means a community has taken a proactive stance to end family violence.

As a survivor of abuse, you can also declare *yourself* a "Domestic Violence–Free Zone." It is a moral stance you can take even if there is still abuse in your life. You are declaring you do not accept being hurt, dehumanized, manipulated, frightened, or controlled. It is a declaration of personal independence from emotional and physical tyranny.

A caveat: Some domestic violence victims are in relationships so dangerous, with abusers who are so violent, that just surviving day to day is a triumph. If you are a woman living in such high risk circumstances, you need to be safe. Please contact your local battered women's shelter immediately for support.

However, if your abusive partner has begun to acknowledge his behavior is wrong and is enrolled in a batterer intervention program, now is the time to insist he end his violence and abuse immediately. It is not your job to fix what has been destroying your relationship—that is *his* work. If your partner is able to sustain his nonviolence over the long haul, perhaps you will choose to continue to be with him. But if he will not change, your commitment to an abuse-free life means you are prepared to proceed without him.

I have watched dozens of women take this stand, and I have seen the courage and strength it brings them. While they may still hope their partner will change (and they may actively support him in his intervention program), they are more focused on their own lives than on saving their relationship or fixing their partner. They no longer are letting their partner hold all the cards or waiting for him to change so that their lives can change. They have resolved to live abuse-free, with or without him.

CHAPTER FOUR

The Last Word:
Voices of Survivors

D OMESTIC ABUSE SURVIVORS ARE my heroines. Not only have they endured and transcended enormous pain in their most intimate relationships but many have gone on to help other abuse victims. The collective effort to end domestic violence would never have the strength, breadth, and power it has were it not for the energy and efforts of survivors. Everything that has made a difference—the shelters and support for victims; the programs for perpetrators; the trainings for law enforcement and the judiciary; the books, films, magazine and newspaper articles; the public education campaigns; the primary prevention programs working with young people—all of these initiatives have been informed and shaped by the experiences of domestic violence survivors.

As I describe in the beginning of the book, my work in the batterer intervention world began with a conversation I had with a survivor. Nancy's husband, Scott, had just begun to address his abusive and controlling behaviors. But it was Nancy's desire to talk to other partners that inspired me to create an outreach and support program for these women. A few years later, when I started working directly with abusive men, I knew I still needed to keep listening to survivors. Their experiences always helped me keep on track. Without their voices, I doubt that our work challenging men and supporting them to change could ever have been as nuanced or deep as it was.

As I was finishing this book, I knew I needed to hear again from survivors. I wanted to be accountable to them. I wanted to know what they thought about the men's stories. Because they are the ones whose lives have been most impacted by abuse, it was important to me that *Unclenching Our Fists* end with their voices.

After I completed the interviews with the men and selected the stories for the book, I organized a focus group of seven domestic abuse survivors and three long-term activists. I invited the women to read a selection of the men's stories and asked them to share their feelings and concerns, including the implications of the stories being published. We gathered in the meeting room of a local battered women's shelter. I explained that I hoped to incorporate our conversation into the book and got their permission to record the discussion which follows below. Unless otherwise indicated, all of the women's names are pseudonyms.

Barbara is in her mid-fifties and works as counselor at a substance abuse facility. She experienced emotional abuse for most of her thirty-year marriage. Her husband attended a batterer intervention program but made only superficial changes. Barbara participated in his program's partner support group. As she became more empowered and realized her husband was never going to make the deep changes she needed, Barbara chose to leave. It was a courageous decision because it was in direct opposition to the teachings of her religion.

Yoko (*her real name*) was a successful clothing designer who retired a few years ago. A longtime activist in the battered women's movement, she has served on the boards of local battered women's shelters, an antiviolence men's center, and a statewide commission addressing victim assistance. Yoko's story is recounted in the preface. Since the tragic deaths of her daughter and grandson, Yoko's efforts have been tireless, both in her home community and state and her native Japan. She has received numerous awards and recognition for her work.

Gloria is the executive director of a battered women's program.

Leslie is a survivor of an emotionally abusive relationship. Her partner attended a batterer intervention program but when he made no changes, Leslie left him. She has one son from that relationship, now a teenager. She works with trauma survivors and is now in a healthy relationship.

Jean has worked with domestic abuse survivors for a quarter century as a hotline counselor, court advocate, and partner-support staff of a batterer intervention program.

Miriam began as a sexual assault counselor and later became the codirector of a battered women's program. For more than a decade and a half, she has worked for the District Attorney's office as head of the domestic violence unit. Miriam has been instrumental in creating a coordinated community response to domestic violence, linking law enforcement and service providers.

Carol was married for more than fifty years. Her husband was verbally abusive for most of the marriage. About six years ago, she started being more assertive and standing up for herself. Her husband became enraged and left the marriage. Carol says she's glad to be out of the relationship, although she struggles to fix some of the damage left in her ex-husband's wake, particularly with her adult children.

Callie is a survivor of a more than thirty-year abusive marriage. She is still with her husband and has seen some changes but not all that she would like. She went back to school to become a therapist and now works with women who've experienced domestic violence.

Louise is in her fifties and married. Her husband has been verbally abusive and was referred to the local batterer intervention program by his therapist. He had made some changes but none that were long lasting. Though Louise is still with him, she agonizes over whether staying in the marriage is the right thing to do.

Pamela has been married for more than fifty years. She says she swept a lot of her husband's verbal abuse under the rug, but "the rug won't take anymore." She has decided it's not too late to try to make things better for herself. At the time of the focus group, she was taking steps to end her marriage.

IT WAS AFTER A long workday when we gathered to share dinner and chat. After eating, the women pushed away their dishes and started reading the men's stories. I gave them three questions to consider:

- What do the men's stories bring up for you on a personal level?
- Is there anything about the stories that brought up concerns, skepticism, or mistrust? Is there anything else would you have liked to hear the men talk about?
- How do you feel about stories like these being the focus of a book? What hopes or fears do you have about the attention these stories might get?

What follows is a summary of our wide-ranging conversation. The women responded not only to the stories they read, but also to the possibility of other abusive men "unclenching their fists."

Barbara: Reading these stories saddens me, because I know that the men in the book represent such a small percentage of men with abuse problems. I think about how many others there are that need to learn these things.

Yoko: I wish we could see a lot more men change the way these men did. That's my biggest concern—how do we reach out to more men? I think this is the key: how do we get to the men who still are abusive and have been for years and years?

Jean: I think part of the solution lies with men who see other men being abusive. I was really glad that James's boss made him go to the group. I wish that would happen more. It would be great if more men who have power would insist that abusive men do something to change. I wish more men in those positions would say, "Hey, you've got a problem, you've got to do something about it."

Miriam: Remember that James would never have gone to his program if he wasn't made to because of his job. It took someone who had more power than him to make him go. If that's the way to get men into programs, it's a start. When James started, he didn't believe in the work. But when he stuck with it, he learned that he needed to be there.

Louise: It would be nice if that could happen in everyday life; if someone sees someone else being abusive—that they would say something and not just walk away.

Leslie: In some of the stories, it felt like they still didn't have much empathy for their partners or former partners. Empathy is so important—it didn't seem like a couple of these guys had it. That was scary for me.

Jean: I found myself feeling impatient as I read all the similar stories about growing up in abusive families. I just wanted to jump to the second half. I understand already about many abusers' backgrounds—I just wanted to see if they really changed. Like, let's get right to it.

Miriam: Yeah, I have no doubt they were abused as children. But at some point, you need to take responsibility. In the first story I read, I didn't see much of that. I felt like at the end I was supposed to feel sorry for him, but I didn't.

Leslie: I was a survivor of domestic violence growing up, but I don't beat people. I was tortured, but I don't treat people the way I was treated. Being exposed to domestic violence in your family is no excuse. In each story, what I saw was this twisted relationship with powerlessness and helplessness. It seems like it really twisted these men up where they ended up inverting it and then projected it out. Seeing that over and over again also made me feel lucky for who I am, that I didn't make those choices. It also reinforces for me, though, that there should be no excuses.

Carol: These stories brought up a lot for me. Like when one of the men talked about how he would blame his partner for everything—that really struck a chord for me. I lived with someone who was always telling me it was my fault. There were constant put-downs. That's a really difficult thing to live with.

Louise: The stories brought up a lot of painful memories for me too. At first I was feeling empathetic for the men. But then I realized . . . that's what keeps me in my relationship. I struggle with this contradiction. I don't want to be an unempathetic person, . . . but where do I draw the line to make things better for me?

Callie: I just felt angry reading the stories. Reading them brings up the same feelings I had when I was in my support group and heard about what the other women were going through.

Gloria: I didn't feel a lot of compassion either. It's hard to find compassion after years of hearing survivor stories.

Pamela: For me it was good to see that there are some men who are willing to do the hard work needed to make changes in their lives. It was encouraging to read that they wanted to make amends. They seemed to realize how their abuse had affected the other people in their lives and realized that saying they were sorry wasn't enough—that they couldn't go back and fix those relationships. So for me it was hopeful—and it means that if these men can do it, then others can do it. The proof is in the pudding, though. It's clear that the work needs to be long term.

Barbara: I had a lot of feelings about that—what a long time it takes to really change. It seems like there really is a middle place— where men know they want to give up their old way of being but they're not yet fully in their new way of being.

Gloria: These stories remind me that this really is a long process; that it takes years of work. It's important that men know that there's a lot more involved than just reading this book—there's no quick fix. They shouldn't expect a Disney ending.

Leslie: Some of the guys seemed further along than others.

Barbara: What about when "Michael" wanted his partner to go over the power and control wheel and show him how *she* was abusive. (*Group laughs*)

Author: It's important to remember that this is not a book about men *completing* their journeys, necessarily, but about men *being* on their journeys. There are stages upon stages of deepening awareness.

Miriam: I felt a little differently about Michael. Even though it was clear to me that he was in a process and not done, I felt like he was more forthcoming, more introspective, more able to say, "Here's what helps me. I know I'm in a process."

Barbara: I was really interested in the places where the stories are so different between partners. It's so clear that perpetrators and victims have such different ways of looking at things. In one story, one of the men talks about being frustrated and throwing his keys. At the same time he tells us that his wife told his mother she thought he was going to kill her. It highlights how differently the perpetrator and the victim experience an incident. . . . I also really liked learning about the things that helped these men change. My favorite part of Michael's story was his description of his bond with his first therapist. It speaks to the importance of having someone believe you can change and the importance of hope. Not false hope—but hope based on truth is so important. I wonder how difficult it was for these men to have any kind of hope for themselves.

Carol: I liked Emiliano's story. It had everything—seeing abuse, living through abuse. For him to come out of that was a real success story.

Leslie: Emiliano's story was very inspiring to me as well. It's clear that his work on himself is integrated into all of his life—all of the areas where he gives back. He is in full service, providing support to other people experiencing domestic violence.

Jean: I appreciate what he said about penance and that he realizes that his silence is what has made other men's violence possible.

Callie: I'm glad you have a chapter in your book about what true accountability looks like because I've seen a lot of what's supposed to be accountability but isn't.

Miriam: I think it will be great for men who are abusive to read this book—to identify with their upbringing, their behavior—to look at what they need to do to change. It can't be stressed enough that the way for them to succeed is to focus on themselves.

Yoko: I think it would be important to include survivor stories, as well as abusers stories. If it's just the abusers stories, I don't know what the people will feel after they've read it.

Leslie: I agree with Yoko. I also want abusive men to read the stories of other men who've changed or are changing. But that's not enough. I also want them to read a survivor's story. I'm concerned about a certain lack of empathy that runs through some of these stories. You can only get that empathy by listening to survivors.

Author: That's absolutely true. It is critical for men working on themselves to hear survivors' stories. In our program, we made sure those voices were heard. Sometimes we had survivors speak to groups, sometimes advocates. Sometimes we showed videos of survivors' stories. That said, I wanted this book to be a chance for all of us to hear about men—the perpetrators—who are changing.

Leslie: I know there may be some controversy about the book among advocates and survivors, but as a survivor I want to say how important it is there's a book like this. Truth is a wonderful thing and the more of it we have of it, the better. Here's a book of men sharing their experiences of trying to change. It's important to get the information out and not worry about how everyone responds. How can we go further if we don't have these stories?

Jean: I'd like to see this book be part of the curriculum of batterer intervention programs. I would love to see guys in batterer programs get a chance to read these stories and critique them. I see this as being really helpful in the field.

Barbara: It's important to understand how change really happens, and what the inner thoughts are of men who are abusive. I was really interested in some of their reflections—like when one guy said, "I never had any friends" or "I had to have a woman to feel complete." If we only approach this issue from the hard line that men need to stop this behavior because it hurts women and children, then we're guilty of making the same error that is made in the context of addiction. "Just say no to drugs" is just a slogan and doesn't express enough understanding about what's going on, what skills people need, and how change happens. That simply can't work with men with abuse issues.

Pamela: I think it's good that hope is one of the messages of this book. So much of the other stuff that's written about domestic violence is pessimistic about change. I think when men read some of those other books; they lose hope that change is possible. I think they have to see some stories of men changing. If abusive men read these stories, it will show them that they can change themselves. I think that's good.

AFTER THE MEETING HAD ended, the feelings the women shared stayed with me for a long time. Their caution, skepticism, sadness, and hope made complete sense to me. I was reminded again of all the ways survivors' lives have been damaged by abuse; for some of them, the damage continues in their relationships with their children or in difficult coparenting arrangements. Reading the stories in *Unclenching Our Fists* brought all those mixed feelings to the surface. Any time an abusive man seemed to sidestep full responsibility or showed a lack of empathy, it triggered understandable feelings of anger. In contrast, when the men demonstrated genuine insight, it brought forward a poignant mixture of hope and sadness for the women in the group: that change is possible, though not for their own relationships.

If there's one thing that men on the journey to nonviolence can learn from survivors, it is that they must steer clear of quick fixes or easy answers. They need to keep peeling back the layers of the onion—to look at how they may still blame their partners or fail to have empathy for them.

If I could have orchestrated it, I would have loved to create a direct dialogue between the men in *Unclenching Our Fists* and the survivors and advocates who responded to their stories. I think one of the best ways perpetrators of abuse can strengthen their capacity for empathy is by listening to survivors. There are very few opportunities for men who've taken responsibility for their abuse to do this. No doubt the conversation would be challenging and difficult. Yet men creating nonviolent lives have so much to learn from women who have experienced domestic violence. And perhaps, survivors as well can gain something from being able to speak with men who are trying to change.

THE FOCUS GROUP WAS not the only way I learned how survivors and advocates felt about *Unclenching Our Fists*. I also asked other advocates to read chapters of the book and to offer their critiques. In addition, whenever possible, I had conversations or correspondence with the current (and in one case, former) partners of the men featured in the book. I wanted to learn how they felt about the book including their partners' stories. I also wanted to make sure that they were still living without abuse or violence.

Of all of those contacts, the one that moved me the most was my brief correspondence with Leta, Dave's ex-wife. As you may recall from his story, he had come frighteningly close to killing her. Dave broke Leta's neck when he pushed her and her head struck the wooden arm of a sofa. A year later, Dave was prosecuted for the assault and sent to prison. It took a long time, but Leta fully recovered from her physical injuries, though the emotional wounds still linger.

My correspondence with Leta was unexpected. By the time I interviewed Dave, he was in the final stages of terminal throat cancer. His medical treatment included surgery that took out part of his tongue. As a result, his speech was garbled. Dave's group leader warned me that though he could still talk, I might need to break the interview into smaller segments, as his voice and energy permitted. Dave knew his remaining time was precious. He insisted we complete the entire interview in one sitting—he would only occasionally stop to sip or spray his mouth with water.

A few weeks after the interview I called Dave back. Although I had recorded our conversation, as I tried to transcribe it, I found I couldn't understand much of his speech. I left Dave a message, but he never returned my call. A month later, Leta left me a voicemail: Dave had died a day before I'd telephoned him.

I immediately called Leta to express my condolences. I knew from Dave's interview that in the past couple of years they had done a lot of healing in their relationship. During our conversation, Leta asked me about the interview and I shared my dilemma: Dave's story was so powerful and I wanted to include it. But many parts of the recording were impossible to understand, I told her. Leta was quiet for a moment and then said something I still find remarkable: she offered to transcribe her ex-husband's tape. She explained that since she had little difficulty understanding Dave, she would be willing to transcribe the interview. I was stunned.

Several months later, I received a package in the mail—a bound transcript filled with pages of single-spaced typing. It had taken Leta more than twenty hours to transcribe the interview. I can only imagine what she must have been feeling as she listened not just to her ex-husband's voice but to Dave's description of his abuse of her and his story of waking up, of changing from one kind of man to another.

Leta had taken an emotionally courageous step. She told me how important it was to her that Dave's story be included in the book. She said it had been worth all the time it took to transcribe the tape; she was proud of the work Dave had done on himself. She was proud, too, she said, of the healing they had done together in the last years of his life.

Leta attached a personal note to the pages of the transcript. It said, "Please remember the victims of abuse. It is easy to forget us so you can move forward with an agenda. Helping abusers is a noble and necessary cause. Please, please remember why you are helping them."

Leta is right, of course. *Unclenching Our Fists* would have little meaning if we failed to remember the victims—like my grandmother, who lived with severe emotional abuse at a time when there were no words for domestic violence, or Leta, who nearly died at the hands of Dave's violence. As we focus on abusive men on the journey to nonviolence, may we always remember why we are doing this work. We want to create a world where no woman or child is afraid of being hurt by the men in their lives. We want to create a world where boys and men can have loving, egalitarian relationships and where they are encouraged to become, as Ron said, "good and gentle men."

Notes

INTRODUCTION

1. Bureau of Justice Statistics, *Special Report: Intimate Partner Violence and Age of Victim, 1993–1999*. US Department of Justice (Washington, D.C., October 2004).

CHAPTER 1

1. Bureau of Justice Statistics, *Special Report: Intimate Partner Violence and Age of Victim, 1993–1999*. US Department of Justice (Washington, D.C., October 2004).
2. Bureau of Justice Statistics, *Intimate Partner Violence in the US*. US Department of Justice (Washington, D.C., 2005).
3. Bureau of Justice Statistics, *National Crime Victimization Survey*. US Department of Justice (Washington, D.C., 2010).
4. Credit must be given to the Domestic Abuse Intervention Project, Duluth, Minnesota, for their pioneering work in developing a model for community coordination in response to domestic violence.
5. Babcock, Julia. "Does Batterers' Treatment Work? A Meta-analytic Review for Domestic Violence Treatment," *Clinical Psychology Review* 23, no. 8 (2004): 1023–53.
6. Edleson, Jeffrey. *Promising Practices with Men Who Batter. Report to King Country Domestic Violence Council* (January 2008).
7. Gondolf, Edward. "Evaluating Batterer Counseling Programs: A Difficult Task Showing Some Effects and Implications." *Aggression and Violent Behavior* 9, no. 6 (2004): 605–631.
8. Aldarondo, Etiony. "Assessing the Efficacy of Batterer Intervention Programs in Context." Discussion paper presented at Batterer Intervention: Doing the Work and Measuring the Progress, sponsored by the National Institute of Justice and the Family Violence Prevention Fund, Washington, D.C., November 2009.
9. Titles mentioned in this chapter are included in the Selected Bibliography at the end of this book.

Acknowledgments

I T "TAKES A VILLAGE" to accomplish most things of significance in life: this book is no exception. Nine years ago, when I was first inspired to collect stories of abusive men who'd committed to change, I had no idea how long and arduous the writing process would be, especially while juggling motherhood and the demands of the rest of my work life. Completing this book has truly been a marathon. I would not be here were it not for the enthusiastic support from my "village" of family, friends, and colleagues. I am grateful to every one of you.

Thank you to Steven Botkin, John Breckenridge, Mark Nickerson, David Thompson, Kevin Ryan and Steve Trudel for giving birth to the Men's Resource Center and the Men Overcoming Violence Program. I am so fortunate to have shared this work with such dedicated colleagues, including Juan Carlos Aréan, Russell Bradbury-Carlin, Rob Okun, Jan Eidelson, Barbara Russell, and my brilliant and compassionate coleader for seven years, Steve Trudel. In addition to sharing the work, they also provided invaluable critiques of the manuscript. Juan Carlos Aréan offered assistance at every stage of this project— helping me find men to interview, offering insight about the research controversies, and reviewing the resource appendix.

I also wish to thank Scott and Nancy Girard, for sharing their lives and struggles and setting my life work into a new and unexpected direction. Thank you also to the seven members of my original Partner Support group, who taught me about process of change and the times when nonviolence isn't enough to heal a relationship scarred by abuse. I also thank Yoko Kato, for inspiring me with her years of committed activism, and Mary Kociela, for her leadership in our community.

Margaret Lobenstine provided invaluable coaching at the beginning of the writing process, helping me organize the book proposal and believing in the importance of this project. I thank the women of Safe Passage for offering meeting space for the important discussion survivors had about the stories in this book.

Many batterer intervention program directors across the country offered their support and connections with men who had been successful in their programs: Alyce LaViolette, Dave Mathews, Heidi Carlson, Rhea Almeida, and Chris Huffine. I thank Lisa Nitsch for her insights about how a detailed description of the process of change could be empowering for abuse victims. Thanks also to others in the field who believed in this project and provided me with an opportunity to speak about the book before it was even published: Lonna Davis, David Garvin, and Ed Berkovich.

I wish to thank David Adams for connecting me to Vanderbilt University Press. Michael Ames, editor at Vanderbilt, has been a champion for this project. Michael understood the complexities and the need for balance between hope and caution and provided remarkable guidance over the four years from proposal to completed manuscript.

I offer my heartfelt gratitude to my local editor and friend, Rob Okun, who spent many Fridays with me at my dining room table revising the manuscript. Thanks to Rob also for getting the word out and gathering support from other authors and activists for this project.

I wish to thank my parents, Saul and Yetta Elinoff, for a lifetime of support and belief in me as a writer. My sister, Lois Rubin, and niece Beth Rubin, authors themselves, encouraged me many times along the way when my enthusiasm was flagging.

My women's group has been with me through this project and through the last seventeen years of life. I can barely imagine who I would be without their love and support. Thank you in particular to Lynne Davis, Sara Schley, and Annette Cycon for such devoted friendship, and to Diane Norman for traveling with me to Utah and for taking the photograph of "Michael."

My husband, Peter Acker, has accompanied me every step of the way, helping me through all phases of this project. He recorded the interviews, offered technical assistance, and never complained about the time I needed away from the family for writing. I am especially grateful for his remarkable portraits, which express the humanity of the men in this book. Peter traveled solo through terrible weather to take photos in Los Angeles and Austin, even though he hates flying! Simply put, I could not have completed this book without his steady love and support.

Finally, I wish to thank my beautiful daughter, Sophie, for being in my life. Her kind and joyful spirit is a daily inspiration. May her own life journey be filled with the safe and loving relationships we all yearn for.

Pelham, Massachusetts
October 24, 2012

Resources

If you are experiencing physical violence or emotional abuse in your relationship, you deserve support. To speak confidentially about your situation and to get help finding a supportive program in your area, please contact the National DV Hotline: 1-800-799-SAFE or *www.the-hotline.org*.

Other web resources for those experiencing abuse:

- National Coalition Against Domestic Violence: *www.ncadv.org*
- National Center on Domestic and Sexual Violence: *www.ncdsv.org*
- Resource Center on Domestic Violence, Child Protection and Custody: *www.ncjfcj.org*

If you recognize you are being abusive to your partner and are looking for help, here's how you can track down a local batterer intervention program:

- All states have domestic violence coalitions that keep a list of resources, including batterer intervention programs. To find the domestic violence coalition in your state, visit *www.ncadv.org/resources/StateCoalitionList.php*.
- Additionally, you can find a list of websites for domestic violence and batterer intervention resources in all fifty states at *www.biscmi.org/other_resources/state_standards.html*.

- You can also contact the local domestic violence program in your area to ask about services for those who use abuse in their relationships.

If you are seeking to learn more about the work of batterer intervention programs, the Batterer Intervention Services Coalition of Michigan (BISCMI) has gathered information about agencies that provide these services, not only in Michigan but across the country. Their website, *www.biscmi.org*, is considered to be the best existing national resource of batterer intervention work. They maintain an updated list of state standards for programs that work with domestic abusers. BISCMI also hosts two conferences each year for batterer intervention practitioners, victim advocates, social workers, and those in the criminal justice system.

Organizations Addressing Violence against Women

- Futures Without Violence (formerly the Family Violence Prevention Fund): *www.futureswithoutviolence.org*
- Battered Women's Justice Project, Criminal and Civil Justice Center: *www.bwjp.org*
- Battered Women's Justice Project, National Clearinghouse for the Defense of Battered Women: *www.ncdbw.org*
- National Resource Center on Domestic Violence: *www.nrcdv.org*
- National Indigenous Women's Resource Center: *www.niwrc.org*
- Mending the Sacred Hoop: *www.mshoop.com*
- National Latin@ Network for Healthy Families and Communities: *www.nationallatinonetwork.org*
- Institute on Domestic Violence in the African-American Community: *www.dvinstitute.org*
- Asian and Pacific Islander Institute on Domestic Violence: *www.apiidv.org*
- National Health Resource Center on Domestic Violence: *www.futureswithoutviolence.org/health*

- National Center on Domestic Violence, Trauma, and Mental Health: *www.nationalcenterdvtraumamh.org*
- National Network to End Domestic Violence: *www.nnedv.org*
- A Call to Men: *www.acalltomen.com*
- Men Against Violence Against Women: *www.mavaw.org*
- Mentors in Violence Prevention: *www.mvpnational.org*
- Men Can Stop Rape: *www.mencanstoprape.org*
- Men's Resources International: *www.mensresourcesinternational.org*
- MenEngage Alliance: *www.menengage.org*
- V Day: *www.vday.org*
- White Ribbon Campaign: *www.whiteribbon.ca*

Selected Bibliography

**For Those Experiencing Abuse
(and Concerned Family Members and Friends)**

Why Does He Do That? Inside the Minds of Angry & Controlling Men.
Bancroft, Lundy. 2003. New York: The Berkley Publishing Group.

The Verbally Abusive Relationship: How to Recognize It and How to Respond,
3rd ed. Evans, Patricia. 2010. Avon, MA: Adams Media Corporation.

Getting Free: You Can End Abuse and Take Back Your Life. NiCarthy, Ginny.
1997. Seattle: Seal Press.

When Love Goes Wrong: What To Do When You Can't Do Anything Right.
Jones, Ann, and Susan Schecter. 1992. New York: HarperCollins.

*The Emotionally Abusive Relationship: How To Stop Being Abused and How
To Stop Abusing.* Engel, Beverly. 2002. Hoboken, NJ: John Wiley & Sons

*Should I Stay or Should I Go?: A Guide to Knowing if Your Relationship
Can—and Should—be Saved.* Bancroft, Lundy, and JAC Patrissi. 2011.
New York: Berkley Books.

*It's My Life Now: Starting Over After an Abusive Relationship or Domestic
Violence.* Dugan, Meg Kennedy, and Roger Hock. 2006. New York:
Routledge.

Healing the Trauma of Domestic Violence: A Workbook for Women. Kubany,
Edward, Mari McCaig, and Janet Laconsay. 2003. Oakland, CA: New
Harbinger Publications.

*When Violence Begins at Home: A Comprehensive Guide to Understanding
and Ending Domestic Abuse.* Wilson, K. J. 2006. Berkeley, CA: Hunter
House.

*Family and Friends Guide to Domestic Violence: How to Listen, Talk and Take
Action When Someone You Care About is Being Abused.* Weiss, Elaine.
2003. Volcano, CA: Volcano Press.

Surviving Domestic Violence: Voices of Women Who Broke Free. Weiss, Elaine.
2004. Volcano, CA: Volcano Press.

For Perpetrators of Abuse

Learning to Live Without Violence: A Handbook for Men. Sonkin, Daniel J., and Michael Durphy. 1997. Volcano, CA: Volcano Press.

Stop Hurting the Woman You Love: Breaking the Cycle of Abusive Behavior. Donaldson, Charlie, Randy Flood, and Elaine Eldridge. 2006. Center City, MN: Hazelden.

Violent No More: Helping Men End Domestic Abuse, Paymar, Michael. 2000. Alameda, CA: Hunter House.

Breaking the Cycle of Abuse: How to Move Beyond Your Past to Create an Abuse-Free Future. Engel, Beverly. 2005. Hoboken, NJ: John Wiley & Sons.

Rage: A Step by Step Guide to Overcoming Explosive Anger. Potter-Efron, Ronald. 2007. Oakland, CA: New Harbinger.

Beyond Anger: A Guide For Men: How to Free Yourself from the Grip of Anger and Get More Out of Life. Harbin, Thomas. 2000. New York: Marlowe & Company.

Fatherhood and Domestic Violence

"Fatherhood and Domestic Violence: Exploring the Role of Men Who Batter in the Lives of Their Children." Williams, Oliver J., Jacquelyn L. Boggess, and Janet Carter. In *Domestic Violence in the Lives of Children: The Future of Research, Intervention, and Social Policy*, edited by Graham-Bermann, Sandra A., and Jeffrey L. Edleson (pp. 157–87). 2001. Washington, D.C.: American Psychological Association.

The Batterer as Parent: Addressing the Impact of Domestic Violence on Family Dynamics. Bancroft, Lundy, Jay Silverman, and Daniel Ritchie. 2012. Thousand Oaks, CA: Sage Publications.

Parenting by Men Who Batter: New Directions for Assessment and Intervention. Edleson, Jeffrey, and Oliver Williams. 2007. New York: Oxford University Press.

High Risk Domestic Violence

Why Do They Kill? Men Who Murder Their Intimate Partners. Adams, David. 2007. Nashville: Vanderbilt University Press.

Assessing Dangerousness: Violence by Batterers and Child Abusers. Campbell, Jacquelyn. 2007. New York: Springer Publishing.

Expanding the Conversation: New Perspectives on Domestic Abuse and Interventions with Perpetrators

Violent Partners: A Breakthrough Plan for Ending the Cycle of Abuse. Mills, Linda. 2008. New York: Basic Books.

Strengths-Based Batterer Intervention: A New Paradigm in Ending Family Violence. Lehmann, Peter, and Catherine Simmons. 2009. New York: Springer Publishing.

Family Violence and Men of Color: Healing the Wounded Male Spirit. Carrillo, Ricardo, and Jerry Tello. 2008. New York: Springer Publishing.

Programs for Men Who Batter: Intervention and Prevention Strategies in a Diverse Society. Aldarondo, Etiony, and Fernando Mederos. 2002. Kingston, NJ: Civic Research Institute.

Books about Men's Socialization

The Macho Paradox: Why Some Men Hurt Women and How All Men Can Help. Katz, Jackson. 2006. Naperville, IL: Sourcebooks.

The Guy's Guide to Feminism. Kaufman, Michael, and Michael Kimmel. 2011. Seattle: Seal Press.

Stiffed: The Betrayal of the American Man. Faludi, Susan. 2000. New York: Harper Perennial.

The Gender Knot: Unraveling Our Patriarchal Legacy. Johnson, Allan. 2005. Philadelphia: Temple University Press.

Guyland: The Perilous World Where Boys Become Men. Kimmel, Michael. 2008. New York: HarperCollins.

Getting Off: Pornography and the End of Masculinity. Jensen, Robert. 2007. Boston: South End Press.

Men's Work: How To Stop the Violence that Tears Our Lives Apart. Kivel, Paul. 1998. Center City, MN: Hazelden.

Reaching Men: Strategies for Preventing Sexist Attitudes, Behaviors and Violence. Funk, Rus. 2006. Indianapolis, IN: JIST Life.

Index

Page numbers in **bold** refer to photographs.